❧ ❧

The words are simple. It's a prayer that millions of people utter every day, all over the world.

But how many of us really understand the eternal words left by Our Lord Jesus Christ?

In this wonderful, practical guide to unlocking the life-changing power of the Lord's Prayer, Terry Fullam analyzes each line and gives us important keys to experiencing God every day.

❧ ❧

Living
The Lord's Prayer

Living The Lord's Prayer

Everett L. Fullam
with
Bob Slosser

BALLANTINE BOOKS • NEW YORK

For Ruth and our children—
Everett, Melanie,
and Andrea.

To Pray the Lord's Prayer
as Jesus intended is to pray for life
as God intended.
To live the Lord's Prayer
is to live in the
will of God

CONTENTS

❧ *Preface* ❧

THIS MIGHT BE a dangerous book, and I believe we should think of that for a moment.

It is a probe into some specific words spoken by Jesus and, for that reason, a probe into the collection of writings from which those words are taken—the Holy Scriptures.

It would be possible to study the Scriptures from several points of view. Some might be interested in them primarily as ancient documents—among the oldest in the world. Or some might hold an historian's interest in the period covered in the various books. Still others turn to them as historians of religion, for they shed much light on that area. It would also be possible to study them from a purely external point of view, examining their sources and development, their structure, their survival as documents.

This book takes none of those approaches, as valid as they might be. Instead, it accepts the Bible's own view of itself: that it proceeds from the mouth of the Lord. God

1

simply chose human agencies—a terribly risky business— to communicate it, having Himself provided the inspiration, the talent, and the occasion. Thus the Scriptures are correctly called the Word of God.

And that is the foundation for this book, which means the reader should understand that the author stands in a circle of commitment. He writes as one committed to the truth of which he speaks, not as one dabbling in ideas.

I am certain there is something eternally significant about any honest examination of the Scriptures. There are mountains of evidence that the Lord God has chosen to bless those who approach Him by opening themselves to His Word. Not to see this raises the danger I mentioned. For as we examine His words, with even a grain of sincerity, we are indeed drawing close to the living God. We even peer into His heart. I believe no one can do this without, in some degree, changing.

Now that is a threatening thought to some people. The possibility that any area of our lives will be changed is threatening, but I suspect that threat becomes more ominous when it deals with our "religious" life than with anything else.

It was October 1, 1972, when I stood before the congregation as rector of St. Paul's Episcopal Church in Darien, Connecticut, for the first time, and I vividly remember telling those people something that turned out to be absolutely true.

I told them that one of two things would happen to them in the days ahead. As the Scriptures were taught and acted upon, they as individuals would find themselves opening more and more to the Lord, growing and maturing. Or they would find the opposite; they would constrict and tighten under the teaching. The atmosphere would become intolerable.

A few did, in fact, leave, but only a few. The others drew closer to the Lord.

God has that effect on people. We cannot deal with His Word very much without having it step on our toes. It points out things like a searchlight and demands a response. That can be dangerous . . . to old ways of life.

EVERETT L. FULLAM
Darien, Connecticut

"Lord, Teach Us to Pray"

CONSIDER FOR A moment that strange assortment of men who nearly 2,000 years ago were called into the fellowship of Jesus Christ as His first disciples. What a motley little crew, you might say: at least four fishermen, a tax collector for the despised occupation government, a zealot burning with desire to throw off the Roman yoke. All were so different.

You can't help but wonder how Matthew the publican got along with Simon the Zealot. They must have been at one another's throat. And there was Peter the hothead, forever speaking first and thinking later. You wonder how he got along with the two "Sons of Thunder"—James and John—whose mother was so ambitious for them.

Yes, they were a diverse group. In fact, about the only thing you can see that tied them together was an overwhelming attraction to the person of Jesus. Somehow, when He said, "Leave your nets, Peter and Andrew and James and John; leave the seat of custom, Matthew; leave your insurrection, Simon, and follow Me," they did.

There was a magnetism about this Man we have come to know as God incarnate. It fairly jumps out at you from the pages of the New Testament. The disciples no doubt observed this dynamism about Him in what He said and did, but there was one segment of His conduct that especially commanded their attention: His prayer life.

The Scripture says that, now and then, He would slip away and spend a whole night in prayer. This man, bursting with life, bursting with purpose, the focus of any group He was in, seemed to find it necessary to break away to be alone with His Father. You can almost hear the disciples talking among themselves: "What is He doing? What is He saying? How can He spend so much time out there alone?"

After awhile they began to suspect that part of the underpinning for the powerful life unfolding before their eyes had to do with those solitary times of prayer. It became clear that Jesus had a link with eternity. Though He moved through time, there was something transtemporal about Him, something in Him that brought people into confrontation with the deep issues of life. I'm sure He was fun to be with—natural and joyful, a good companion—but somehow His manner and His words tended to pitch people's attention onto important things, matters of depth and permanence. He was a man with one foot planted in time—for God truly intersected history with His incarnation—but with the other foot in eternity.

Now we have to remember that these were Jews. Prayer was not new to them; they undoubtedly said prayers themselves. But in Jesus they observed a communication with the Father that was somehow different.

So it is not surprising that St. Luke recorded the moment when the disciples went to Jesus and said, "Lord, teach us to pray.[1] Teach us the secret of your powerful life. How do you do it?"

It's interesting that Jesus didn't go to *them* and exhort them to prayer. He let the Holy Spirit open their eyes a bit. He waited until they had detected the importance of prayer in His life before He began to talk about it. But when they asked, He responded.

That response is found in its most familiar form in the sixth chapter of Matthew's gospel and is probably the best known passage in the Bible. We call it the Lord's Prayer, although that is a misnomer. The episode in the 17th chapter of John's gospel—where, on the night before His suffering, Jesus poured out His heart to the Father—is really the Lord's Prayer. The passage in Matthew would be more aptly called "the disciples' prayer."

People who know nothing else about the Bible can often recite this prayer. It's a part of church services, repeated routinely week after week around the world. And that is one of the great tragedies of the Christian church, because to miss the truth of the Lord's Prayer is to miss much of what Jesus had to say about life itself. For Jesus wasn't setting forth something merely to be recited as part of a liturgy. He was setting forth a way of life. I am convinced that to understand the Lord's Prayer and to pray it in absolute sincerity is to embrace a whole concept of being. It addresses every aspect of our life.

To pray the Lord's Prayer as Jesus intended is to pray for life as God intended. To live the Lord's Prayer is to live in the will of God.

The prayer itself is short, a mere 68 words in the form most common to the church today. A moderately paced recitation requires about half a minute. But those words contain the secrets of life. They are capable of bringing immense fulfillment—to the person praying and those being prayed for. And they will bring joy to Almighty God.

They contain the secrets to the kind of life every man or woman of integrity desires whether he or she acknowledges it or not. I know it's the kind of life I desire with every ounce of my being.

* * *

1. Luke 11:1 ff

We need to see immediately that Jesus' answer to His disciples was not a pat formula. That was not His habit. He was not saying, "Now here is a 68-word prayer that you can use." Neither was He saying, "You must pray these words just this way."

I am convinced He did not intend for His followers to repeat this prayer word for word every time they gathered. And that is not to say there is anything wrong with reciting the Lord's Prayer when we meet. I merely believe this was not Christ's primary purpose. He was showing the disciples the best approach to prayer—a pattern if you will. He was giving the priorities in prayer, and thus the priorities in life—a distillation, really, of His whole teaching while on earth.

It's as though He was saying to His disciples, once they'd asked, "Okay then, if you want to pray, well, pray like this . . ."

You might say Jesus let the disciples look at His notes on prayer. He let them see His outline. I suspect this is the outline or order He used when He went off by Himself to talk to the Father.

I believe He was saying, "Do you want to pray for 10 minutes? Then pray this way. Do you want to pray all night? Then pray this way." His outline can be infinitely expanded, even to cover a week of fasting and prayer.

I remember once, a long, long time ago, when I decided to pray all night. It simply seemed like a good thing to do. Well, I set out, and I prayed, and I prayed, and I prayed. Oh, did I pray! Then I looked at my watch. Five minutes had passed. I couldn't believe it. So I prayed some more. I prayed everything I could think of; I prayed some things twice. I looked at my watch again. Five more minutes had passed. And I had exhausted everything I knew to pray about. I was worn out. There was no way I could pray all night.

Since then the Holy Spirit has opened my eyes to the reality of the Lord's teaching on prayer, and I now find it thoroughly feasible and delightful to pray through the hours or the days or the nights—whatever seems best.

"If you want to pray well," Jesus said, "then pray this way..."

Precisely because His prayer is so well known, there is a pitfall: it can become a series of empty phrases. Many of us have reached that dreadful point where we can recite the whole prayer and not have a single word sink into our hearts and minds. We can recite it while thinking about something entirely different. I deplore those times when I've repeated the Lord's Prayer during a service while planning the day's activities.

Certainly, that is the first thing Jesus wanted us to avoid. Before giving the disciples the prayer, He cautioned them:

> "...when you pray, you must not be like the hypocrites; for they love to stand and pray in the synagogues and at the street corners, that they may be seen by men. Truly, I say to you, they have their reward. But when you pray, go into your room and shut the door and pray to your Father who is in secret; and your Father who sees in secret will reward you.
>
> "And in praying do not heap up empty phrases as the Gentiles do; for they think that they will be heard for their many words. Do not be like them, for your Father knows what you need before you ask Him."[2]

A hypocrite, of course, is someone who poses as one thing while in fact is being something else. He is greatly concerned with his image, with how he looks to other people, with how he's coming across.

People who pray prayers just the way they're supposed to be prayed, externally, but with little thought about what they're praying, can fall into that category. Their religion becomes a matter of going through motions. They can sing hymns, listen to Scripture readings, kneel at the proper times and never worship God They can even receive the sacra-

---

2. Matthew 6:5-8

ments in a manner that accomplishes nothing—nothing pleasing to God and nothing beneficial to themselves.

The only reward for such conduct, Jesus was saying, comes from whatever esteem or recognition others of similar mind might bestow.

Instead He instructed His disciples to go into their own rooms—into their "closets," according to the early English translations. For us a closet is a place where one hangs clothes, but for the people of the first century it was a little shed attached to a house, a place where food and other things were stored—a pantry. There one could go and be unobserved.

"When you pray," Jesus said, "go into such a room, for the God who sees in secret will hear you."

In my particular branch of the body of Christ, the Episcopal Church, we should be especially aware of the futility of public posing. For we regularly begin our service of Holy Communion by addressing the Lord this way:

Almighty God, unto whom all hearts are open, all desires known and from whom no secrets are hid...

The One we are dealing with penetrates the external postures and sees the heart. He simply is not impressed by how beautifully we do the liturgy; He is not impressed by how we look and act on the outside.

So Jesus said, "If you want to pray correctly, there must be no posturing."

This was not a new thought regarding God. The Jews of Christ's time knew it despite their practices; it was plain in their Scriptures.

Chapter sixteen of First Samuel shows how the Lord felt about a new king for His people. He sent Samuel the prophet down to the little town of Bethlehem with directions to proclaim a public sacrifice and invite all the people, especially Jesse and his sons, "for I have provided for myself a king among his sons."[3]

---

3. I Samuel 16:1

On the appointed day, the sons of Jesse approached the altar, each bringing his sacrifice, and Samuel stood back thinking to himself, *I wonder if this is the one?* or *Is it that one?*

Finally, one of the sons, Eliab, approached. The Scripture says he stood head and shoulders above everyone, handsome and regal. "Surely this is the Lord's anointed," Samuel said. But God spoke to him the same lesson taught by Jesus:

... "Do not look on his appearance or on the height of his stature, because I have rejected him; for the Lord sees not as man sees; man looks on the outward appearance, but the Lord looks on the heart."[4]

And, of course, young David was ultimately chosen—the one who had a heart after God. As Jesus was saying, Almighty God, never fooled by outward appearances as men so often are, makes His judgments through an infallible understanding of the heart. He sees us as we really are.

The fact is driven home for us when we see how David, in turn, dealt with his successor:

"And you, Solomon my son, know the God of your father, and serve him with a whole heart and with a willing mind; for the Lord searches all hearts, and understands every plan and thought."[5]

Nothing escapes the Lord—a fact running throughout the Bible. A New Testament writer said it this way:

And before Him no creature is hidden, but all are open and laid bare to the eyes of Him with whom we have to do.[6]

---

4. I Samuel 16:7

5. I Chronicles 28:9

6. Hebrews 4:13

So Jesus' point was sharp as He taught His disciples how to pray. God sees hypocrisy instantly and despises it.

This does not mean, of course, that Jesus was opposing public prayer. Scripture is perfectly clear in showing that God's people are to assemble frequently and to pray aloud when they do. The point is that *everything* done toward God must proceed from the heart. Merely following the rules outwardly will not suffice. "If your heart isn't in it," Jesus was saying, "then you might as well not do it."

Nor does Christ's warning about "too many words" mean God doesn't want me to share everything with Him. It would be a misunderstanding to conclude, "Well, since God knows everything, including what's in my heart, why bother to tell Him all these things? Why belabor Him with facts He already knows? I'll just be piling up empty phrases." That misses the point. God wants me to share all of life with Him, but He wants all of me while I'm doing it, not merely my pious words.

One thing I have noticed about myself over the years is that, as my prayer life has become more profound through better comprehension of the teachings of Jesus, my prayers have in fact become shorter. I don't mean to suggest that as a requisite. But for a long time I served as something of an adviser to the Almighty. I never offered a prayer without instructing the Lord exactly how and when to answer it. I offered Him much advice about the conduct of the universe, most of which, fortunately, He let pass.

I was a good deal like a woman I heard start a prayer by asking, "Lord, did you see the news tonight?"

Eventually I found that the more I submitted to the Holy Spirit and to the lordship of Jesus in all the details of my life, the less I was impelled to instruct God about anything. That, of course, didn't mean I stopped taking everything before Him. It merely meant I realized that answers no longer depended on my solving everything.

"Your Father knows what you need before you ask Him," Jesus said.

"Then," some might respond, "why bother to ask?"

12

Probably the best reply is that the Lord has *told* us to bring all our concerns and burdens to Him:

"Come to Me, all who labor and are heavy laden . . ."[7]

Why should He say such a thing? The answer lies in God's primary purpose for us, who are every bit as diverse as those first disciples. He wants to build a relationship, that of child to father.

"If you then, who are evil, know how to give good gifts to your children, how much more will your Father who is in heaven give good gifts to those who ask Him!"[8]

It seems obvious that the Lord is perfecting an attitude in His people. When the disciples came to Him and said, "Teach us to pray," He, above all others, knew that what they asked was impossible. One can't be taught to pray. One can be taught to *say* prayers, even to memorize them, and one can be shown a guideline or pattern for prayer.

"If you want to pray well, then pray this way . . ."

---

7. Matthew 11:28
8. Matthew 7:11

❧ One ❧

Our Father

IF YOU LOOK at the Lord's Prayer closely, you will see it is divided into two parts, with six petitions in all. The first three have to do with God—with hallowing His name, with seeking His kingdom. The second three have to do with *our* needs. And in these we are directed to bring our entire lives—past, present, future—before the Godhead. We are to approach God in such a way as to call upon Father, Son and Holy Spirit, placing the fullness of our lives before the fullness of God.

But there is an order to it. And this was primary to Jesus as He showed us the way to a total experience.

J. B. Phillips, in the introduction to his marvelous little book, *Your God Is Too Small,* said, "The trouble with many people today is that they have not found a God big enough for modern needs." Too often, he said, their understanding of God has not stayed apace with their awe over the exploding universe. They're stuck with a Sunday school conception of the Creator that their own experience denies, worshiping or pretending to worship a God "who is really too small to command...adult loyalty and cooperation."

In short, they have missed the God revealed by Jesus,

the One perfectly capable of handling the complexities of our lives—past, present and future.

In showing us how to approach this God who created everything that exists, Jesus, as always, went right to the point. He simply didn't have a lot of time on earth and so He struck at the heart of every situation. Since the New Testament doesn't pretend to report every minute of every day in the life of Christ, we'll have to get filled in on these details at another time. But in those cryptic exchanges recorded for us, Jesus spoke huge amounts in a single breath: "You must be born again," "I am the bread of life," "No one comes to the Father but by Me." Each sentence was jammed with truth that often would not be fully grasped for years, even centuries.

So it was with the Lord's Prayer. Its 68 words are bursting with meaning, with instruction, with life itself.

Even the first two can stagger us: "Our Father." That is a mouthful.

Remember that this instruction was given to committed followers, not the curious, the mockers, the half-hearted. It was not a public teaching. He had left the crowds and gone up on the mountain with only His disciples.

"Our Father" forces us to see that the Lord's Prayer is not some universal prayer for just anyone. Neither is it a child's prayer, as so many well-meaning mothers and Sunday school teachers try to make it. It is a disciples' prayer: it is for people who call God "Father."

Thus right at the beginning Jesus challenges the tendency in the world today to say that God is everyone's Father. God *is* the Creator of everyone and everything; we people *are* His creatures. But Jesus wasn't talking about that. God is not everyone's Father. Rather, He is the Father of those who love Him and do His will.

The Lord made this plain when He told some religious leaders that their father was not God but the devil. "If God were your Father," He added, "you would love Me."[1] Not

---

1. John 8:42-44

everyone meets that qualification, and the Lord's Prayer is for those who do. "Our Father" set forth not only the person the disciples were addressing but also who *they* were.

Indeed, those words set forth far more than we can imagine.

*   *   *

It was mid-July in 1969, and I was more than a hundred miles into the interior of Liberia. The place was so remote that the residents had not even heard the name Africa, let alone America. The time is easy to pinpoint, for while I was there man took his first step on the moon. I remember listening to a Voice of America broadcast of that astounding event on my little portable radio. What a contradiction to my surroundings!

That afternoon I went to see the chief of the Gheo tribe; his grandson, who had become a friend, served as interpreter. I remember remarking that it was a great day in human history. Two Americans—Armstrong and Aldrin—had walked on the moon.

The old man looked hard into my face. Then he looked up at the moon, visible as the day slipped toward dusk.

"There's nobody up there!" he burst out. He sounded almost angry. "Besides that, it's not big enough for two people to stand on."

He meant it. He had absolutely no conception of the size of the moon or its distance from the earth. Yet it was there in that raw, backward section of the small west African nation that I had one of my most memorable experiences, driving home to me what it means to know God as Father. The moment came when I was invited to baptize three converts from paganism, people who had come to know the love of the Father through the grace of Jesus Christ, although they, like the old chief, knew little about science and the universe.

There were two men and one woman. We stood on the banks of a muddy river, wet and happy. I had never seen three more joyful people.

"What is the best thing about this experience?" I asked.

All three continued to smile, the glistening water emphasizing the brightness of their dark-skinned faces; but only one spoke, in clear, deliberate English: "Behind this universe stands one God, not a great number of warring spirits, as we had always believed, but one God. And that God loves me."

The revelation had broken through. Images of horror and confusion that had filled this African's understanding since childhood had been wiped away. As mysterious and unpredictable as the universe might seem, behind it stood one God, loving it, governing it and caring about him.

Those three Africans could pray, "Our Father." They had a new relationship permitting it. And that relationship settled the one with the unseen world which has perplexed and frightened man throughout history. They knew who they were now, and they knew what the essence of their new world was. God was Father.

But uncivilized cultures are not alone in producing hideous understandings of the unseen world. Greek legend, for example, tells us of Prometheus, said to have lived in a time before the discovery of fire. He took pity on the human race and stole fire from the gods to give to man. What happened? Zeus, the king of the gods, was furious. How dare this upstart offer help to mortal man? So Prometheus was chained to a rock in the Adriatic Sea to suffer under the hot sun and cold nights. Further, Zeus fashioned a hawk that flew at Prometheus and ate his liver. The liver would grow back, and the hawk would eat it again, constantly tearing at Prometheus' flesh. Whether in "primitive" cultures or "enlightened" civilizations, the gods of paganism are terrifying beings. The philosopher Lessing spoke for much of mankind when he wrestled with the nature of the universe. Were he allowed to ask only one question of the Sphinx, considered in ancient times to be a source of wisdom, it would be this, he said: "What is behind the universe? Is it hostile, indifferent, or friendly?"

To pray as Jesus taught settles the question; the terror

and confusion are removed. For His follower realizes that the unseen world is governed by one God. "Furthermore," Jesus says, "that God is your Father." You know where you stand.

Jesus also pointed to our relationship to the *seen* world in the opening words of His prayer. For as His people look at nature around us, we know that behind it, too, stands the omnipotent God who called it into being. This means that no part of the universe, however vast it may be—and it reaches far beyond our imaginations—is alien to us if we know God as Father. It may be distant; it may be unreachable. But behind it, in full control of it, stands the same one God. He fashioned the vast expanses, and he fashioned the environment around us, the place where we live, even the bodies in which we live.

And that all-powerful being is the One Jesus enables us to perceive as "Our Father."

*   *   *

Let's take a closer look at our relationship with "Our Father."

Scripture tells us God created man in His own image.[2] There are animals and heavenly beings, but man alone stands in peculiar relationship to God. He was fashioned in the likeness of the Almighty Himself. This does not mean physical likeness, obviously, since the same Scripture teaches us that God is spirit.[3] So we cannot resemble Him in a corporeal way.

Rather, this means there is a special connection between the infinite God and His finite creation at the point of man. It means, if understood reverently, that man is created in God's class. We are not God; we are not creatures. But our relationship is unique.

Scripture establishes that we, mankind, are creatures of

2. Genesis 1:26
3. John 4:24

God's delight, reflecting His nature, His characteristics. He is spirit; so are we. And that means we can have communion and fellowship with Him.[4]

It is necessary to pursue the revelation, however, and see that this distinct relationship was marred.[5] Adam and Eve turned from what they knew to be right, as every one of us has done at one time or another, with the result that God, with whom they had walked before in peace and love, suddenly became a figure of fear, like the gods of paganism. So Adam and Eve hid themselves.

Ever since that act man has not felt at ease with God, knowing within his innermost self that his existence is marred.

This fact is critical to a proper understanding of the Lord's Prayer, indeed, of the whole Bible. We have no geniune perception until we understand that in our natural condition we are not as God would have us. We have used the gift of freedom in ways contrary to His purpose. We have many times put our wills in the place of His will, causing estrangement between Him and His special creation. We are alienated from the source of our being and, as a result, from our neighbors and even from ourselves. Conflict fills the earth.

Fortunately, man is not separated from God's love. For against this tragic background, Jesus Christ entered the world, coming to restore the relationship, to reconcile man to the Father, to re-establish the "family" tie.

> ... to all who *received* Him, who *believed* in His name, He gave power to become *children of God;* who were born, not of blood nor of the will of the flesh nor of the will of man, but of God.[6]

Through Jesus, God went a step beyond the Garden of Eden. He opened the way to plant His own Spirit, His own

---

4. I John 1:3
5. Genesis 2:15-3:12
6. John 1:12

Life, within us. That Life is not there otherwise, for the Scripture teaches that by nature we are children of wrath[7] and darkness.[8] Jesus Himself was born without human generation, being conceived by the Holy Spirit, and something like that has to happen to those who would enter the family of God. We must be born again[9] by the action of God.

Scripture reveals that this depends not only on believing in Jesus but also on *receiving* Him, which is a matter of decision involving the free will God gave us when He created man in His image. Even Satan *believed* Jesus was the Son of God.

It is this restoration through Jesus that we acknowledge and confirm when we venture into the Lord's Prayer. We pray uselessly if this is not our intention.

* * *

"Our Father" takes us even deeper than that, however. Jesus' words urge us to recall the quality of that relationship as taught by St. Paul:

> ...all who are led by the Spirit of God are sons of God. For you did not receive the spirit of slavery to fall back into fear, but you have received the spirit of sonship.[10]

He challenges us quite simply: Do we run and hide at the thought of God? Are we slaves under orders—do this, do that, or else? Does our God thunder down from Mount Sinai? Or are we walking with Him in the spirit of sonship? For St. Paul declares:

> When we cry, "Abba! Father!" it is the Spirit himself bearing witness with our spirit that we are children of God...[11]

---

7. Ephesians 2:3
8. I Peter 2:9
9. John 3:3
10. Romans 8:14-15
11. Romans 8:15-16

I've had people say to me, "But I've never cried Abba, Father." The only answer I have is, "Well, maybe you should." For "abba" is an Aramaic word of great endearment. The closest we can come to it in English is "daddy." I've always thought it odd that translators don't usually translate it.

When a baby begins to talk, one of the first things he says is "da-da." And in the English-speaking world, we fathers get all flustered and excited, thumping our chests with pride and bragging, "Hey look, he's talking to me!" I remember when all three of my children for the first time said "da-da." I loved it.

In the Middle East, however, the random syllables that bring this parental response are "ab-ba." They mean the same thing in the Semitic world as our "da-da" does. "Abba, ab-ba," the child gurgles.

And the Scripture tells us that when we cry, "Abba, Father... Daddy, Father," the Spirit of God convinces us inwardly that we really are His children.

This is the mouthful that our Lord Jesus Christ was uttering when He instructed His disciples to pray, "Our Father." It has the most profound meaning in the world. Each of us needs to ask himself: Do I have the kind of relationship with God that makes me want to crawl up into His lap, as it were, and say, "Daddy"? Do I feel that close to Him? Or is God beyond my reach, way out there in eternity somewhere, remote and withdrawn? Has He come down only as far as Sinai, where He hands down commandments and laws? Is He someone who tells me only what I can and cannot do?

That's not the God Jesus was revealing. He was showing forth the One who has given His people His very own Spirit—Himself—to convince them deep down inside that they indeed are *more* than His people. They are His *children!* He wants them to cry instinctively to him, "Daddy... Abba... Father."

The Bible uses two metaphors to show us how God achieves this: birth and adoption. At times it speaks of our being "born" again by the Spirit of God. At others it insists that Jesus is actually the only begotten Son of the Father,[12] and we are more properly "adopted" into the family.

St. Paul, summarizing the religious development of Israel, wrote that,

> ... when the time had fully come, God sent forth His son ..., to redeem those who were under the law, so that we might receive adoption as sons.[13]

What an astounding act! He has given His people individually the same Spirit who was in and upon His Son, Jesus Christ, when He was on earth; the same Spirit Who motivated the Lord when He went off into the hills to pray, Who stirred Him to cry, "My Father! My Father! Abba!" He has planted something of His own nature within them even though they are merely adopted.

*　　*　　*

We may not like to hear it, but the New Testament shows there is no genuine prayer until this father-child relationship is established, until one is born into the family of God or, to use another analogy, is adopted and sealed by the Spirit. People can be taught to *say* prayers, to *read* prayers, to *memorize* prayers, but they cannot be taught to *pray*. When the relationship exists, they pray instinctively. Anything else is mere words. That is what Jesus was teaching.

David du Plessis, the grand old man who has carried the message of the renewal and unity from nation to nation and church to church for the last 30 years, has reminded us pointedly that "God has no grandchildren." We can't have this wonderful relationship on the basis of godly parents or a life of churchgoing. We can't be grandchildren, or cousins, or nephews; God only has children, born through faith.

---

12. John 1:14
13. Galatians 4:4-5

At a service not long ago in Washington, D.C., a woman approached me to pray with her for a deeper walk with the Lord. So I asked, "Have you committed your life to Jesus Christ? Have you been born again by the Spirit?"

She tightened her lips in quiet desperation, and she blurted, "I'm trying!"

And that was her problem. How does one *try* to be a son? He either is or isn't. I never worked at being a Fullam. Never in my life did I try to be the son of my parents. I tried to be a good one occasionally, but that's as far as I could go. For it takes no effort to be a son.

So many people lose sight of that when they approach God. They try to squeeze themselves into such a relationship by earning His favor, when the only issue is, have you opened the door of your life to Jesus Christ? That can be answered yes or no. If you have, then all you need to remember is:

> . . . in Christ Jesus you are all sons of God, through faith.[14]

There is one other word in this opening phrase of the outline Jesus laid down for His disciples: "Our." Jesus said, "Our Father," not "My Father." This is a *family* matter. The Christian life is a collective life, a community life.

We Christians need this awareness today, for we are too often infected with an independence growing out of our secular roots that tends to glorify rugged individualism. There is no room for this in the church as described in the New Testament. The church is shown to be a body, a family—with diversity for sure, but not independence.

*   *   *

So we see how the Lord would have His people begin to seek Him. There is only one way, He said, and that is

---

14. Galatians 3:26

through a Father-child relationship. It does no good to embark on prayer until that issue has been decided. But once it has been settled, once we have been born again by the Spirit of God, prayer becomes as natural as breathing, and we see indeed that the beginning, the approach, for everything in life is "Our Father." Are you seeking God's will for something in your life? Begin with "Our Father."

After these words, it doesn't matter how incoherent, how desperate the cry. It will be spoken into the ear of God, for He sees the heart and recognizes the voice of His own child, much as a mother can recognize the cry of her child in the middle of a nursery of screaming children.

⪧ *Two* ⪦

Who Art in Heaven

IMAGINE YOU HAVE a blackboard in front of you, and we have drawn a line across it halfway between the bottom and the top. Everything below the line represents the world within our experience—the absolute limit of our human reasoning, even of imagination. Then we place the Lord God above that line, beyond the reach of human knowledge, wisdom, understanding. Our finite minds will not penetrate that area, no matter how hard we try.

Now this would be a true picture were it not for the astounding fact, the most central and sobering teaching of the Christian faith, that God at a real point in history came down below that line and entered the world of our experience. In this boundless universe of galaxies, quasars and formations surpassing our wildest imaginations, this tiny little globe on which we live became, in the words of J. B. Phillips, "the visited planet." God Himself, in the person of His Son, came among us.

What we can know about God is what He deigned to show and tell us. And even then, because the language we use was fashioned in this world, it is only by extreme stretching that we can talk about Him at all.

Jesus faced this; the writers of Scripture faced it. We face it when we humbly pray, "Our Father, who art in heaven."

We see more clearly the problem of trying to talk about things above that imaginary line in John's description in the revelation of his great vision of the heavenly city.[1] "It has something like streets of gold," he said in effect.

Obviously he was not saying that the streets were made of literal gold. He was trying to put into words we could understand something of the splendor of what he had seen. John said, similarly, "The gates are like pearls." Again, he was simply using an expression from the world of our experience to describe something we cannot comprehend.

The Scripture writers had an even more difficult time before the incarnation. Think of the problem of talking about the God who appeared to Abraham, Isaac, Jacob, Moses and the prophets. They were limited to earthly descriptions of a heavenly being, falling back on things like, "The Lord is my shepherd."[2] Obviously, the Lord is not really a shepherd; He's something *like* a shepherd. And we get a glimmer of understanding from that. Or they said, "The Lord is a rock."[3] Now they did not mean that God is a stone. They were saying that He has some of the characteristics of a rock in that He is durable and unfailing, always there, impenetrable. And when they said He was "a devouring fire,"[4] readers understood. If you put a piece of paper in a fire, it is consumed. "Well," they said, "the Lord, who is a jealous God, can be something like that."

The "hand" of God reaches down, stretches out, and touches; the "arms" of God shelter us; His "ear" is attentive to our prayer; His "eye" roves to and fro upon the earth.

---

1. Revelation 21:1-22:5
2. Psalm 23:1
3. Psalm 19:14
4. Deuteronomy 4:24

We don't know how God sees, hears and touches, but the only way we can talk about Him is to use the finite to describe the infinite.

Even the notion of God as "father" is born of human experience ascribed to Him only by analogy. And Jesus taught we should do this. In the entire Old Testament God is referred to as Father only six times and then rather impersonally. But in the gospels, which together are only a small fraction of the length of the Old Testament, Jesus speaks of God as "my Father" or "our Father" more than 60 times. And because of our human experience, we can understand the term, catching a glimpse of the nature of Almighty God. We understand a father to be one through whom life is begotten. He is also a provider, a protector of the family. God is like that.

And since we're drawing on our earthly experience, many people hit a snag. Some have had unworthy fathers. Some have been so hurt and scarred that it is unsatisfactory for them to think of God as father.

We had a minister from the strife-ridden Bedford-Stuyvesant ghetto of Brooklyn visiting our affluent parish one weekend who drove this point home.

"In the culture in which I grew up," he said, "there were hardly any fathers to be found. There were always children, everywhere, and there were women, married and unmarried, but there were no fathers—or very few. They had left, run out, split. To talk about the love of a father is completely alien to such children. It's somethng totally lacking in their experience, and preaching on it has no impact on them, at least positively."

Even in St. Paul's parish the word "father" doesn't always produce the desired picture. Our children come from comfortable homes, but some rate second best in the competition for their father's attention. Jobs, social status and other things come first. As a result, many aren't really clear on what a loving father is all about.

Jesus, of course, understands this, so in the Lord's Prayer He says, "Our Father *who art in heaven*." He strips away all limitations we might place on the word "father" because of our human experience. He wants us to see Him as absolutely unlimited, infinite, unfettered by restrictions our lives in the world might tend to place on Him—heavenly, not earthly. He wants us to see that He is omnipotent, omniscient and omnipresent, although our experience renders us incapable of fully comprehending those descriptions.

Finally, He wants us to see that we are not bound by any tragic experiences with earthly fathers. For, no matter how good our home lives may have been, our human fathers were finite creatures; they had limitations, often serious ones. They sometimes failed in their understanding and comprehension, in their patience, their endurance, their consistency. He wants to lift us above that.

So Jesus said, in effect, "When you pray, say, 'Our Father,' for God is something like that. But also say 'who art in heaven,' knowing truly that you are talking to the One who has no limitations. He's your Father, but He's the transcendent One."

*　　*　　*

The Lord wanted His disciples to gain a perspective on life that human eyes alone will not give. "You are to pray—and live—with eyes of faith," he said in essence. "You are to see what cannot be seen by the eyes of men."

We are to go above that imaginary line—if not with our language, at least with our faith, the faith described by the writer of the letter of the Hebrews:

Now faith is the assurance of things hoped for, the conviction of things not seen.[5]

There are many examples of this seeing with the eyes of faith in the history of God's people. Elisha provided one when the Lord revealed to him how the king of Syria was

---

5. Hebrews 11:1

going to ambush the Israelites.[6] The king sent a great army to capture Elisha and put an end to the frustration of his war effort:

> When the servant of the man of God rose early in the morning and went out, behold, an army with horses and chariots was round about the city. And the servant said, "Alas, my master! What shall we do?" He said, "Fear not, *for those who are with us are more than those who are with them.*"

Now that was an observation made with the eyes of faith. The two Israelites were surrounded. But Elisha knew that the forces of Almighty God, the One *who is in heaven*, were greater than the forces of the enemy. His God had no limitation. And he wanted his servant to have that perception.

> Then Elisha prayed, and said, "O Lord, I pray Thee, open his eyes that he may see." So the Lord opened the eyes of the young man, and he saw; and behold, the mountain was full of horses and chariots of fire round about Elisha.

Do you see the difference? Elisha's helper, looking with human eyes, did not see the host of heaven protecting the servant of the Lord. He saw only the enemy. He hadn't a clue as to what was really going on. So Elisha prayed and soon the young man had eyes of faith; he knew with Whom he was dealing.

And that is precisely what we need when we pray, indeed when we live. So many times the situation seems humanly impossible, but we must lift our eyes above it, as Jesus said, to "Our Father, *who art in heaven.*"

*　　*　　*

6. II Kings 6:8-18

When Jesus spoke of the Father in heaven He was looking to the realm where God's power is totally without limitation. He wants us to look there when we pray to remind ourselves that we are dealing with a Being who knows everything while we do not. He is the One in Whom we place our faith. We can trust Him, the infinite One.

A thrilling passage in the book of the Revelation reveals why this works. The scene is heaven.

> After this I looked, and lo, in heaven an open door! And the first voice . . . said, "Come up hither, and I will show you what must take place after this." At once I was in the Spirit, and lo, a throne stood in heaven, with One seated on the throne![7]

It helps to close your eyes and allow yourself to be transported along with John to that perspective. He had been earthbound before. True, he had been looking up to God, but there came a point when he heard a voice that said, "I've got something I want to show you *up here*." And in one of Scripture's most majestic moments, he entered in the Spirit into the throne room of the universe.

He saw that, although Rome was in power, although the emperors breathed fire and hatred against the Christians, there was a throne in the universe and the Lord God was upon it, not the emperors. He learned at that moment, and wrote it down for those who followed, that we must never think for a second that God loses control of the world. We must never fail to see through to that throne room.

Centuries before the coming of Jesus, God revealed through the prophet Micah that the Messiah would be born in Bethlehem.

> But you, O Bethlehem Ephrathah,
>   who are little to be among the clans of Judah,

---

7. Revelation 4:1-2

---

from you shall come forth for me
    one who is to be ruler in Israel . . .[8]

But when the time came, it appeared there had been a mistake. The angel of the Lord went not to Bethlehem, but to Nazareth, to confront a young maiden: "Mary, the Spirit of the Lord will hover over you and that which shall be conceived in you shall be called the Son of God." (Luke records this in the first chapter of his gospel.) The earthbound mind immediately says, "This is all wrong! The prophets have made a mistake."

Meanwhile, the Emperor Tiberius was merrily sunning himself on the Isle of Capri when the thought popped into his head: "I think I'll take a census. I'll have every family return to its hometown for it." So he issued a decree, moving Mary and Joseph from Nazareth down to Bethlehem, the hometown of Joseph's lineage, at the right time for the exact fulfillment of the prophecy.

It all seemed so natural. Only from the control room of the universe, as it were, was the true picture seen. Only from there could it be perceived that Tiberius' thoughts had been put into his mind by the One who governs everything.

Yes, God sits on the throne. Kings rise and fall at His behest. All power exists *under* Him.

And we, His people, are depending on Him, the One who is not baffled by that which baffles us. He expects us to turn to Him and say, "Father, you know the end from the beginning. Nothing exceeds your greatness. Thy will be done in my life, now and forever."

With that clearly fixed, we can pray—and live.

---

8. Micah 5:2

≥ Three ≤

Hallowed Be Thy Name

I'VE NOTICED SOMETHING about myself and many other large men. A little problem in some rather insignificant part can put the whole body out of sorts. A pain in the finger, for example, can get blown all out of proportion with me. I can hardly function. Or at least I *think* I can hardly function, and that thought dominates everything else. It can become the center of everything.

The small needs that press in on all of us daily are like that. They can dominate our existence, distorting life and actually taking control. One result is that prayer often becomes a rush into God's presence in the white heat of our need and a demand that He do this or that, that He bless this and the other thing, that He help us.

Although we might deny it, prayer can become our instructions to the Lord on what should be done. We even fill in the tiniest details, as though He might have missed something, perhaps while taking a nap. We start by presuming we understand something He doesn't; we know our needs and those of the ones for whom we pray, and we must explain them to Him. In this way prayer can be a matter of getting God to do our bidding.

It's remarkable that the Lord understands even about little finger pains that get blown out of proportion; and He pays attention to us. We *are* His children and He never forgets it, despite our impatience and narrow understanding of circumstances. He is concerned about our personal needs and desires, no matter how small, and He wants us to talk to Him about them, even though He already knows them.

But let's get our priorities straight according to the teaching of Jesus. He told us: "The first petition you are to address to our Father, if you are to pray rightly, does not concern your own needs. It concerns Him. Proper prayer begins with a desire that the name of God be hallowed."

Remember, the first half of the prayer Jesus used to instruct His disciples had nothing to do with their individual needs. It dealt with the concerns of God. The lesson is that, when we turn to the Lord and involve ourselves in His concerns first, somehow the problems that so overheated us seem to shrink. We begin to see with His perspective.

So we worship Him, and we dwell in His presence. We do not have to invoke that presence for He never goes away; He never turns His back on us.

"... I am with you always, to the close of the age."[1]

We simply begin by turning to Him, opening ourselves to His presence, positioning ourselves under his sovereignty, basking in His light, reflecting on His awesome acts, simply glorifying His name.

"Hallowed be Thy name." All prayer should begin that way, Jesus said.

* * *

Why are we so concerned about the *name* of God?

The Bible tells us that the names of persons are very significant.

---

1. Matthew 28:20

Consider Abraham. He was first called Abram, which meant "exalted father." But God, after calling him, altered his name to Abraham, which meant "father of a multitude." He was to be the father of a "multitude of nations."[2]

And there was Jacob. His name meant "deceiver, cheat, swindler," and Scripture tells us he lived up to that name. But the time came when God intervened, changing Jacob's name to Israel, which meant "prince with God." He was turned from a swindler and cheat into royalty with God.

So holy was the name of God to Jews of old that they refused to pronounce it. When they read the Scriptures aloud, they did not say the word, which consisted of four consonants, transliterated JHWH, which later became Jehovah or Yahweh. When they came upon the name, they substituted the word Adonai, which means Lord. Generally, in the English translations of the Bible the word Lord was initially the unpronounceable name.

We see numerous references in the Scriptures to "thy name":

...those who know *thy name* put their trust in thee...[3]

"Those who know Thy name" seemingly could mean those who simply know that His name is Yahweh. But no, the name of God stands for the whole being of God. To know His name is to know His character, personality, His temperament, His love, His mercy, His power.

The psalmist sums it up when he states that, "Those who truly know who and what You are put their trust in You." And also...

Some boast of chariots, and some of horses; but we boast of the name of the Lord our God.[4]

---

2. Genesis 17:5
3. Psalm 9:10
4. Psalm 20:7

As we walk in the Lord's name, as we walk with Him, the clearer that name becomes. For He reveals Himself to us in the circumstances of our lives, a fact corresponding perfectly to the progressive nature of His written revelation, the Scripture. He never has revealed everything about Himself or His will at one time, nor does He do so now.

In Genesis we read this:

> When Abram was ninety-nine years old the Lord appeared to Abram, and said to him, "I am *God Almighty* (El Shaddai) . . ."[5]

The gods of the pagan nations, with whom Abraham was familiar, were called *mighty* gods, but here God revealed Himself as the *Almighty*. Four hundred years or so later, He added to that revelation in an exchange with Moses:

> ". . . I am *the Lord* (Yahweh). I appeared to Abraham, to Isaac, and to Jacob, as God Almighty, but by my name the Lord I did not make myself known to them."[6]

The three patriarchs had understood Him as God Almighty, but there was more. There was the one and only God, the eternal God, the "I AM,"[7] the God of the unspeakable name—Yahweh—and that name was made known in the circumstances lived through by Moses just as the many names of God are revealed to us as we walk with Him. He doesn't change; He merely shows us more of Himself as we hallow His name.

Later in the Exodus story, we find the people of Israel wandering in a wilderness, coming at last to a watering spot. But the water was brackish and couldn't be drunk. Moses cried to the Lord who responded by showing him a

---

5. Genesis 17:1
6. Exodus 6:2-3
7. Exodus 3:14

---

tree to throw into the water, and the water became sweet and healthful.

> There the Lord made for them a statue and an ordinance and there He proved them, saying, "If you will diligently hearken to the voice of the Lord your God, and do that which is right in His eyes, and give heed to His commandments and keep all His statutes, I will put none of the diseases upon you which I put upon the Egyptians; for I am the Lord, *your healer.*"[8]

For the first time they knew another name of their God: Healer. The understanding came through crisis.

Later the Israelites came up against the Amalekites, a fierce tribe that didn't want the Israelites in their land. So they attacked. Moses went up on a mountain and began to pray with hands lifted high. As long as his hands were raised in a sign of total dependence upon the Lord, the Israelites prevailed. But when he tired and lowered his hands, the Amalekites triumphed. Finally, Aaron and Hur held his arms so he could pray until the Israelites were victorious.

> And the Lord said to Moses, "Write this as a memorial in a book and recite it in the ears of Joshua, that I will utterly blot out the remembrance of Amalek from under heaven." And Moses built an altar and called the name of it, *The Lord is my banner* ...[9]

In a perilous situation where Israel prevailed only through calling on His name, God revealed something else about Himself. "I'm your banner," He said. "I'm the rallying banner under which you march forward and do battle against your enemies." Another word for banner in this instance is "victory," a name learned in the crucible of experience.

A new name for God shone forth when Gideon encoun-

8. Exodus 15:25-26
9. Exodus 17:14-15

tered an angel of the Lord. He didn't know who it was at first and was afraid. But soon the light dawned.

> Then Gideon perceived that he was the angel of the Lord; and Gideon said, "Alas, O Lord God! For now I have seen the angel of the Lord face to face." But the Lord said to him, "Peace be to you; do not fear, you shall not die." Then Gideon built an altar there to the Lord, and called it, *The Lord is peace.*[10]

Abraham discovered one of the most encompassing names of God in a terrifying encounter over his only son, Isaac, born to his wife, Sarah, in their old age. When the boy was 12 or 13, a staggering word came from the Lord:

> "...Take your son, your only son Isaac, whom you love, and go to the land of Moriah, and offer him there as a burnt offering upon one of the mountains of which I shall tell you."[11]

Can you feel the horror that struck in Abraham's heart? He didn't even tell Sarah about it. But he took one or two servants and his young son and left early in the morning. They reached the mountain, and only Abraham and Isaac climbed it, Isaac bearing the wood on which he was to be sacrificed.

Part way up the mountain, the child turned to his father. "Dad, we have the wood and the fire, but where's the sacrifice?"

Abraham said softly, "The Lord will provide Himself a sacrifice."

They reached the top and Isaac helped his father build an altar. Then Abraham took his son, tied him and put him in place. He raised the knife.

"Don't touch him!" It was the Lord. "I never intended

---

10. Judges 6:22-24
11. Genesis 22:2

for you to take the life of your child. I wanted to see if you would obey me."

At that moment they turned and saw a ram caught by its horns in a thicket. The sacrifice had been provided, as Abraham had said, although history now causes us to read his remark, "God will provide Himself *as* the sacrifice." For it pointed to the future. On that very mountain, Jesus many years later carried His own cross and died, bearing the sin of the world.

Abraham glimpsed something of this and learned an additional name of God from the greatest crisis of his life.

So Abraham called the name of that place *The Lord will provide* . . . [12]

"Hallowed be Thy name" recalls that marvelous truth about our Father.

Writing more than 700 years before Christ, the prophet Isaiah foresaw something unusual about the name of God:

For to us a child is born,
    to us a son is given;
and the government will be upon His shoulder,
    and *His name will be called*
"Wonderful Counselor, Mighty God,
Everlasting Father, Prince of Peace." [13]

He understood something new, and it points us directly to the New Testament:

". . . and you shall call His name Jesus, for He will save His people from their sins." [14]

---

12. Genesis 22:14
13. Isaiah 9:6
14. Matthew 1:21

Jesus means "Yahweh saves" or "Yahweh is salvation." And in the anxiety of his experience, Joseph heard an angel of the Lord name God the Son as the savior of His people.

The apostles, too, learned about the name of God. The book of Acts tells us of a healing accomplished under the ministry of Peter and John that created a stir. Peter told the people they shouldn't wonder or stare as though the two of them had healed the man. He pointed to Jesus:

> "...And *His name*, by faith in His name, has made this man strong..."[15]

Later Peter said:

> "And there is salvation in no one else, for *there is no other name under heaven given among men by which we must be saved.*"[16]

And St. Paul spoke similarly, declaring that Jesus Christ had been raised

> far above all rule and authority and power and dominion, and *above every name that is named*, not only in this age but also in that which is to come...[17]

It is important that we see the level to which the Scripture exalts and hallows the name of God and especially the name of Jesus. Many people in our churches—especially in my own branch of the body of Christ, the Episcopal Church—are relatively comfortable with the word "God" or even "Lord." But they are uneasy with the name "Jesus."

"It's so personal," they say.

But the Father exalts it, the Scripture exalts it. How can the church not exalt it?

---

15. Acts 3:16
16. Acts 4:12
17. Ephesians 1:21

Jesus said we should hallow the name of God, and this takes on richer meaning as we walk with Him, learning what His name really is—God, Lord, Healer, Victory, Peace, Provider, Savior. And above all is the name of Jesus.

As we move through life, our depth in hallowing God's name will increase as these dimensions are included. The Lord Himself will fill His name with more content, and as we pray and live in the manner outlined by Jesus, we will remember that content and will pray and live in the love, joy, peace—and power—intended for us.

But, having examined "the name" of the Lord, we are left with the word "hallow." What precisely do we express when we say, "Hallowed be Thy name"?

The word means "to make holy or set apart for holy use; to respect greatly." It means to avoid use in a common way.

We begin to understand it by examining the second commandment:

"You shall not take the name of the Lord your God in vain..."[18]

That does not refer to profanity, although it would be included, of course. Basically, it means, "Don't use the name of God in an empty and thoughtless way."

I found myself earlier in life frequently saying, "O Lord this" and "O Lord that," simply as part of my regular speech. It wasn't profanity; it was idle talk. And one day the Lord convicted me about it. I was using His name in a careless and thoughtless way, just as the second commandment warned against. I was failing to hallow the name of God, to set it apart in reverence and to regard it as a name to be used in worship and praise.

Thus we see that hallowing the name of the Lord is the other side of the second commandment. It is the positive

18. Exodus 20:7

expression of a negative statement: "You shall not use the name of your God in a vain, thoughtless or empty way; rather, you shall hallow the name of the Lord."

To hallow also means to magnify, to enlarge in significance, to esteem. We hallow the name by lifting it up, by speaking it forth worshipfully and respectfully with its fullest meaning. Indeed, the way to hallow the name of the Lord is to worship and praise Him, to remind yourself of His glory, His great exploits on behalf of the forefathers as well as yourself.

Scripture shows us what the holy men of old did when they turned to the Lord. As recorded in the book of Nehemiah, in the midst of great difficulty, they set the stage for a mighty prayer meeting with the people of Israel fasting in sackcloth as they assembled.[19] They read from the Scriptures for a fourth of the day, which is a significant Bible lesson by any standard. Then they "made confession" and worshiped the Lord for another fourth of the day. The people were told to

"stand up and bless the Lord your God from everlasting to everlasting. Blessed be Thy glorious name which is exalted above all blessing and praise."

And then the prayer itself began:

...Ezra said: "Thou art the Lord, Thou alone; Thou hast made heaven, the heaven of heavens, with all their host, the earth and all that is on it, the seas and all that is in them; and Thou preservest all of them; and the host of heaven worships Thee. Thou art the Lord, the God who didst choose Abram and bring him forth out of Ur of the Chaldeans and give him the name Abraham..."

19. Nehemiah 9:3-32

First, he magnified the name of the Creator, then retold the history of the people of God, beginning with Abraham and running through the covenant, the deliverance from Egypt, the Law and Commandments, the sin of the people, and finally he prayed this:

> "Now therefore, our God, the great and mighty and terrible God, who keepest covenant and steadfast love, let not all the hardship seem little to Thee that has come upon us . . ."

His petitions regarding his needs came far down the line.

There is something remarkable about this. When we, like Ezra, come before the Lord, burdened as we might be with our needs and concerns, a seesaw effect occurs. Our petitions are on one end, and they are elevated in our eyes. But, as we begin to pray, worshiping and praising the Lord, recalling His loving kindness as seen in His mighty acts, setting apart His name, the seesaw begins to work, and our burning concerns are lowered to their proper perspective. The things of God rise to the heights. Praise literally overwhelms our problems.

* * *

In the church where I serve, we have found that hallowing the name of the Lord is as important as anything we do. We make sure we take a lot of time in every service to worship.

At one of our Tuesday morning services which are attended by people traveling great distances, we heard a testimony from a man that cast new light on the subject. As he told it, his wife, having found her way to our church for the first time, immediately discerned a concern and love among the people and felt encouraged to share her heavy burden: she had been told her husband was going to die from a rare disease in the legs. She asked for prayer, which was offered, but in the context of worship; it flowed from praise. The Lord's name was hallowed.

A week later she returned to report that the doctors had said they were going to amputate his legs and try to save his life. We worshiped and praised and prayed some more.

The next week she came back and said, "Well, because they were planning to amputate his legs, they decided to try an unusual thing. They literally split his legs open from hip to ankle—both of them—preparatory to trying a rare treatment. The next day the doctor came in to supervise the removal of the bandages. He looked, and his legs were healed!"

It was an astounding moment. The doctor asked, "What happened to your legs?"

The husband, practically dumb-stricken, blurted out, "I don't know!" He stared at his legs. "All I know is that we have been praying—and they have been healed!"

The man filled in the details for us that Tuesday morning, confirming what the Lord had been teaching us. Healing had been given in the context of praise. Those had not been healing services, obviously—but rather worship services. We had taken our minds off ourselves and our problems and thrown ourselves totally into hallowing the name of the Lord, exalting Him above all. We had discovered the correctness of expecting the Lord, in such a health-filled atmosphere, to bestow gifts of healing upon His people as we acted under His sovereignty.

Similarly, I saw the healing power of worship during a trip to the Middle East. My brother, Rex, was with me. He is a motorcycle fanatic and just a few years earlier had come through an accident that nearly crippled him in the legs. His right arm was seriously damaged, and in the years following he had been unable to raise the arm above shoulder height. He could pull it up with the left one, but it would not function by itself.

In a service of praise in Jerusalem, people around Rex began to lift their hands over their heads in worship and adoration. My brother apparently forgot himself and lifted both hands high. Suddenly he realized what he was doing and dropped them. Then, very tentatively, he lifted the right one, and it went all the way up. There was no pain; the arm was healed.

Rex couldn't believe it. He was a new Christian and knew about such things, but this was a new experience. He had not asked for healing. He had merely hallowed the name of the Lord.

That's what Jesus was telling His disciples. If you want to pray rightly, He said, if you want to live rightly, then pray like this. It will give you the right perspective. It will put your prayers and your lives in order.

❧ Four ❧

Thy Kingdom Come

SURPRISINGLY FEW CHRISTIANS realize it is the purpose of God to establish a kingdom on this earth, a kingdom that will ultimately supplant the kingdoms and nations of this world, a kingdom that will produce righteousness, where the will of God is perfectly done. This blindness to God's goal is unfortunate, and He would have us remedy it.

If we were to search out the single concept that ties all of Scripture together, it would be the concept of the kingdom. Several themes run through God's revelation, but none is more pervasive than that. It is clearly a subject from Genesis to Revelation: God is establishing on earth a sphere of sovereignty, and He is going to great lengths to bring people into that sphere. They are people who will live willingly under His authority, who will relinquish dominion over their own lives and will subject themselves to the Lord of the kingdom who is Jesus Christ.

So it is not unusual to find Jesus mentioning the kingdom prominently when He gave His disciples an outline of how to pray properly. It was the second of six petitions, indeed the centerpiece of that outline. "Pray like this," He said:

> Our Father, who art in heaven,
> Hallowed be Thy name.
> *Thy kingdom come . . .*

He wasted no time in getting to it, for it is primary in God's plan. And He wanted us to put God's concerns first.

The immediacy turns us to the first words of Christ's public ministry as found in Matthew's gospel:

> ". . . Repent, for the *kingdom* of heaven is at hand."[1]

St. Mark recorded it this way:

> ". . . The time is fulfilled, and the *kingdom* of God is at hand; repent, and believe in the gospel."[2]

We see, too, that many of the parables Jesus used in His ministry began with the words, "The kingdom of God is like . . ." And one of His most quoted statements was:

> ". . . seek *first* His *kingdom* and His righteousness, and all these things shall be yours as well."[3]

After His crucifixion and resurrection, He pressed on with the theme:

> . . . He presented Himself alive after His passion by many proofs, appearing to them during forty days, and speaking of the kingdom of God.[4]

---

1. Matthew 4:17
2. Mark 1:15
3. Matthew 6:33
4. Acts 1:3

Jesus taught that if we were to pray rightly we should pray ardently for the kingdom to come. What is this kingdom?

*   *   *

The opening chapters of Genesis record that God created all things, that everything in heaven and on earth owes its existence to Him. And that creation is described as though He accomplished it over a series of days, though it seems clear we are not to understand this as 24 hour periods of time. "Day" has another meaning. As we know, the length of our day of 24 hours comes from the relationship of the earth and the sun. According to the creation account, the sun was not made until the fourth "day," so whatever else that tells us, it apparently is not dealing with 24-hour periods but perhaps with vast stretches of time. We do not know. We often use the word "day" in the sense of "age" or "era," and St. Peter reminds us that "with the Lord one day is as a thousand years, and a thousand years as one day."[5]

Genesis does tell us without ambiguity that God created *all* things. It doesn't give a scientific account of those origins; it wasn't intended for that. It also tells us there was apparently some kind of progression in creation: there was life in the sea before there was life on land; there was plant life before animal life; there was animal life before human life. And that accords with the best and most honest scientific information man has come up with.

I've never understood those who pose a conflict between the opening chapters of Genesis and the deliberations of science. Science does not give us an account of origin, only of development. Even the notion of evolution presupposes something to "evolute" or change. It is not a theory of origins but of development. Whether true or not, it doesn't degrade God and His purpose for man.

---

5. II Peter 3:8

In the first chapter, we are introduced to a momentous thought about that purpose:

> Then God said, "Let us make man in our image, after our likeness; and let them have dominion over the fish of the sea, and over the birds of the air, and over the cattle, and over every creeping thing that creeps upon the earth." So God created man in His own image, in the image of God he created him; male and female he created them. And God blessed them, and God said to them, "Be fruitful and multiply, and fill the earth and subdue it . . ."[6]

Man is shown as the apex of God's creation, brought forth on the sixth day. The words "in our image," however, are actually beyond our grasp. After all, God is spirit, Jesus said, so we do not resemble Him physically as a child might resemble his father. The truth is much deeper, for whatever else it might mean it tells us there is a definite link between man and his Creator. If God is a spiritual being, then so are we. We have physical bodies, and that's important, but we were created for a relationship with God which the Bible calls communion and fellowship.[7]

*   *   *

Think of household pets. I love animals and have always had cats and dogs around my house. They have an affection for me, and I've had wonderful enjoyment from them. But there is a limitation to our relationship. Cats and dogs are an entirely different order of being from man. And although they can express a kind of affection, it is clear that the possibilities for communion and fellowship with them are limited.

God had different plans for Himself and man; He made

6. Genesis 1:26-28
7. I John 1:3

us something like Himself. There is a special bond between us.

He also gave us a special job: "... let them have dominion..." We were created to have a limited sovereignty over all creation, put in the position of overlords or stewards, a job defined as managing the property and affairs of someone else. We were to have dominion over the earth, to bring it under control, to unlock its secrets, to develop the intelligence given to us for this purpose:

> The Lord God took the man and put him in the garden of Eden to *till it and keep it.*[8]

But there was a condition:

> ... the Lord God commanded the man, saying, "You may freely eat of every tree of the garden; but of the tree of the knowledge of good and evil you shall not eat, for in the day that you eat of it you shall die."[9]

At that point man faced the first test of his willingness to live under lordship. And he failed. He attempted to usurp the authority of Almighty God, his Creator. First Eve, enticed by the evil one, and then Adam, her husband, ate from the forbidden tree, and a strange new emotion was introduced into the universe: fear. They had formerly walked with God in harmony and openness, but

> Then the eyes of both were opened, and they knew that they were naked...[10]

They were suddenly intensely aware of their disobedience and their nakedness, a vivid reminder that we, too, stand uncovered before God. Our nakedness causes shame, ren-

---

8. Genesis 2:15
9. Genesis 2:16-17
10. Genesis 3:7

dering us terribly vulnerable before the eyes of God. We are like Adam and Eve who felt it for the first time the moment they disobeyed. They hid.

> "...I heard the sound of Thee in the garden, and *I was afraid,* because I was naked; and I *hid* myself."[11]

Their fellowship had been broken by fear and separation.

The closest Satan, the serpent, ever came to telling the truth was in the garden when he said that if they ate of the forbidden tree they would become "like God."[12] Why? Because the moment the man uses his will contrary to the will of God, the Lord is dethroned from His rightful place as God, and man elevates himself to that place. He assumes the prerogative to determine right and wrong. God said it was wrong to eat from the tree. Adam and Eve said, "No, it is *not* wrong; it is *right.*"

They, with all of us following their example, became the standard by which good and evil, right and wrong, are judged. We exercise our freedom against the will and purpose of God. We establish *rival kingdoms* in which we are the sovereigns, trying to bend others to our wills and purposes. Thus throughout the earth we have millions of kingdoms rival to the kingdom of God, people who will not live willingly under His sovereignty. And we have chaos.

So Jesus said we should pray, *"Thy kingdom come..."*

*　　*　　*

After the disobedience of Adam and Eve, the rest of Scripture tells of God's steps to rescue man. It is a story of restoration, not in the sense of going back to the beginning, but of restoring the perfect state—the original kingdom that man was given to live in forever.

We are to bring forth a kingdom on this earth yet not *of*

---

11. Genesis 3:10
12. Genesis 3:5

this earth, not built or maintained by worldly methods. Jesus said, "My kingship is not of this world."[13] It is not a government conducted by the hand or the might of man. People are not dragged into it. It is a voluntary kingdom, one that refuses to violate the freedom given to man. Its supreme power, its rule, is in the hearts of its people.

The Bible says God's kingdom will one day bring all the kingdoms of the world to the feet of Jesus, replacing them with the kingdom of God and His Christ. We see the first hint of this in what scholars call the "proto evangel," the first mention of the gospel in the Scripture. It is only a glimpse, given immediately after man's fall in the blistering words addressed by God to the serpent:

"Because you have done this . . .
I will put enmity between you and the woman,
    and between your seed and her seed;
He shall bruise your head,
    and you shall bruise His heel."[14]

God was to intervene; He was to bring into the world through the woman a human being, apparently, who would bruise the head of Satan while being dealt a lesser blow.

Next we find Abraham learning that God would intervene through his descendants to bring forth One who would bless the earth.[15] Then we see that narrowed through Jacob, who was renamed Israel, with the indication that that One would have kingly power, symbolized by the scepter:

The scepter shall not depart from Judah,
    nor the ruler's staff from between his feet,
until He comes to whom it belongs;
    and to Him shall be the obedience of
    the peoples.[16]

---

13. John 18:36
14. Genesis 3:14-15
15. Genesis 12:1-3
16. Genesis 49:10

We learn that this kingly One will be from the family of David, His throne will last forever, and He shall be God's son.[17] More precisely, He will be born in the hometown of David, Bethlehem.[18]

Then in the New Testament we find the prophecies, delivered centuries earlier, being fulfilled:

> And the angel said to her, "Do not be afraid, Mary, for you have found favor with God. And behold, you will conceive in your womb and bear a son, and you shall call His name Jesus.
> He will be great, and will be called
>   the Son of the Most High;
> and the Lord God will give to Him
>   the throne of His father David,
> and He will reign over the house of
>   Jacob forever;
> and of His kingdom there will be no
>   end."[19]

When Jesus, at the age of 30, began His public ministry, He proclaimed, as we've noted, that the time was fulfilled; the kingdom of God was there:

> "Fear not, little flock, for it is your Father's good pleasure to give you the kingdom . . ."[20]

And yet, we see more. There is a future, glimpsed by John, the author of the book of the Revelation, and it is toward this that the people of God are aimed:

> To Him who loves us and has freed us from our sins by His blood and *made us a kingdom,* priests to

---

17. I Chronicles 17:11-14
18. Micah 5:2
19. Luke 1:30-33
20. Luke 12:32

His God and Father, to Him be glory and dominion for ever and ever. Amen. Behold, He is coming with the clouds, and every eye will see Him...[21]

It is to all of this that Jesus directed our attention when He told us we should pray, "Thy kingdom come..." He instructed us to be concerned in our prayers and in our lives first and foremost with the kingdom. All of our thoughts, our words, our deeds should move toward that, for it is at the very heart of God.

But let's be precise. What is a kingdom?

It is a sphere of sovereignty, of rule, and it has a king. We must not become ethereal. There is a realm in which God is King and, despite the fact that it is voluntary and not of this world, operating instead in our hearts, it exists now, with visible results. It is not mythical. The King must rule in actuality, not in theory.

At the close of the age, there will be a change in this kingdom. But it exists at this moment.

The question each of us must ask is: Does it rule me?

---

21. Revelation 1:5-7

❧ Five ❧

Thy Will Be Done,
on Earth as It Is
in Heaven

"THY KINGDOM COME" is not a petition meant to
stand alone. Jesus intended it to be linked immediately with
the one that follows:

"Thy will be done, on earth as it is in heaven."

One illuminates the other. The meaning of "Thy kingdom
come" is seen through "Thy will be done," and the breadth
of it is perceived in the phrase that follows, "on earth as it
is in heaven."

To ask that "Thy will be done" is to ask that "Thy kingdom come." It is to ask that God's rule be established in
the hearts, the wills, of men, women and children everywhere. Such rule is the coming of the kingdom at this point
in history. There will be a consummation referred to by St.
Peter as entering into "the *eternal kingdom* of our Lord and
Savior Jesus Christ"[1] but that awaits the return of Jesus
Christ and the close of the age.

---

1. II Peter 1:11

Remember Jesus said His kingdom was not of this world—not in the style of earthly kingdoms. It is within us. So we are to understand that He is calling for the establishment of the unique rule of God on earth now—in the hearts and lives of His people. It is to resemble the rule of God in heaven at this moment.

This leads us to define the kingdom of God this way: it is that state of affairs, that condition, where the will of God is perfectly done.

Do you want to live in His kingdom? Then you must do His will. It should be the continual concern of your heart.

That sounds overwhelming, even impossible, but the Lord does not intend it to be so. His intention could be paraphrased like this: "If you want to pray rightly, to live rightly, you can if your major concern is for your heavenly Father's will to be done on this earth."

That is the first giant step toward living in the will of God.

* * *

Many Christians think God's desire is to make us, His people, miserable. With heads hanging low, we finally sob, "All right, Lord, Thy will be done. I give up." And we throw ourselves upon Him, grit our teeth and wait for the worst. We are inwardly convinced that the place of peace, joy and happiness cannot possibly be the center of God's will. After all, whoever heard of a happy Christian?

The truth is that God's will is that certain place where we will find the peace that passes understanding. It is the place where we will find the joy that is inexhaustible. St. Paul described it:

> . . . the kingdom of God (is) . . . righteousness and peace and joy in the Holy Spirit . . .[2]

---

2. Romans 14:17

As we approach the Lord with our prayers and with our lives—"Thy will be done, O Lord, on earth as it is in heaven"—we are not asking Him to do anything other than His will and purpose. We are not seeking to persuade Him to our point of view.

We see the point vividly in Jesus' words about His own life:

"My food is to do the will of Him who sent me . . ."[3]

That was His entire purpose. "I feed, I exist, on nothing other than the will of God." It mattered not what that will was, for He was the perfect embodiment of life under lordship. He illustrated in His incarnate life what it meant to live in the kingdom of God, always submitted to the authority of the Father, always seeking to find His will and to fulfill it, never attempting to persuade Him contrary to His will.

* * *

If we keep asking, "How can I know the will of God?" we need to see that there is something wrong with the way the question is asked. For the Bible never indicates that the will of God is a problem of knowledge. We can be sure that if God expects us to *do* His will, He will make it possible for us to *know* it. It is a matter of *willingness*. We find a clue to this in Christ's answer to those who questioned whether His teaching came from God:

". . . if any man's will is to do His (the Father's) will, he shall know . . ."[4]

Willingness to do the will of God, He said, is the precondition for discerning that will. As long as we view it as

---

3. John 4:34
4. John 7:17

one of several options, we have trouble. For instance, if I have a decision to make, I can determine what my wife thinks I should do, what my best friend thinks, what my boss thinks and so on, and then lay the ideas out like a cafeteria of options, adding incidentally what I think the will of God might be. And then I can consider them all together. But that won't do. The will of God is not to be thought of as one option among others.

I have found that the Lord will withhold any certainty as to His will in a situation until I have surrendered and decided that I will do His will no matter what it is. My attitude must be: "Lord, I embrace Your will without knowing what it is."

Next we must understand that God has revealed His will in Scripture on many matters, but we often ignore this. Because most of us don't know the Bible very well, we don't realize how much He has revealed through the prophets, the apostles and His own Son, the Lord Jesus Christ.

Take the matter of being unequally yoked. Scripture says clearly that when a Christian marries, he or she is to marry only within the faith. Many times I've had young people come and say they want to know God's will about marrying so-and-so, who turns out to be a nonbeliever. I can tell them they do not need to pray, for He has already spoken.[5] Such a marriage would unite citizens of two kingdoms, functioning under two sovereigns. There would be conflict with inevitable suffering.

Or consider the matter of how much we should give to the Lord. The Old Testament lays down the principle of the tithe as belonging to God—one tenth of what one has. Indeed the Scripture uses the phrase "tithes and offerings,"[6] and the point seems to be that until the tithes that belong to God are paid, there is no such thing as an offering. Having this standard, there is no need to seek God's will about how much to give.

---

5. II Corinthians 6:14-15
6. Malachi 3:8

But what about those things we can't find in the Bible? People have various techniques for trying to determine the right path, and it helps to look at them.

There are fleeces. And Gideon, whose story is found in the book of Judges, was the number one fleece-maker. You will remember that he was preparing to do battle against the Midianites[7] and said, "Lord, if You want me to go up against the Midianites, this is what I want You to do: I'm going to take a fleece of wool and put it here outside my tent, and in the morning I want the fleece to be wet, but the ground dry—if You want me to go up to battle."

That is putting out a fleece.

The next morning, Gideon rushed out of his tent, picked up the fleece, wrung it, and water poured forth. But the surrounding ground was dry.

"Interesting," he muttered, stroking his chin whiskers. "I wonder—I wonder if that just *happened*. Was it a coincidence?"

Then he spoke up to the Lord. "Now, Lord, don't be angry with me, but I'm not sure. That may have been a coincidence. Ah, this is what I want You to do: tonight, I'm going to put it out again. And this time I want You to make the ground wet and keep the fleece dry. Don't be angry, Lord."

And God, in His graciousness, arranged the next morning for the ground to be wet and the fleece dry.

That is the approach many people take with God today. They seek to determine God's will by saying, "If You want me to do it, then let this happen." And every once in awhile the Lord will come around and do it that way. But you can almost see the frown on His face. It is not a good way, certainly not the best. The reason is simple: we experimenters, being very human and frail and subject to temptation,

---

7. Judges 6:36-40

act just the way Gideon did. We wonder and doubt and question whether the result is just coincidence or whether God did indeed answer. No, the way of Gideon's fleece is not included in Scripture, in my judgment, as an example of the right way to seek God's will today. It is most likely included to show how trying we can be to the Lord.

Then there are open doors. Sometimes people say, "Well, the thing to do to follow God's will is to go where there are open doors. If God opens a door, go through it; if He closes it, stop."

Several things are wrong with that approach. The most obvious is that the whole thing breaks down if you have more than one open door. You find yourself standing there, glancing nervously from one to the other, frustration mounting, faith ebbing.

Also, God sometimes leads us up against closed doors or blank walls. Several men in our parish provide good examples. They were moving along in the will of God, seeking Him, following Him, serving Him faithfully in the fellowship. Their families were blossoming. Suddenly disaster struck. In one of the nation's economic throbs, their jobs were wiped out, and they faced a blank wall. There was no place to go, no door to walk through. It wasn't that the doors closed; there just weren't any doors. Their lives seemed to grind to a halt. And yet I know, both through faith and through the results, that those men had been moving in the will of God. He led them to blank walls, and they remained blank for many months. As they stood helplessly in front of the blank walls and cried out painfully, "What is the will of God for me?" it would have been cruel for someone to say, "Well, find an open door and go through it." There were no open doors. Did that mean they were out of God's will? I do not believe so.

Thus I'm not able to accept the open-door and closed-door principle as the perfect way.

There is always the casting of lots. In the book of Acts we see the disciples trying to pick a successor to Judas

Iscariot.[8] They cast lots. First, they chose two men, Joseph called Barsabbas, who was surnamed Justus, and Matthias. Then they said, "Lord, You know the hearts of these men and whichever one You want, You choose." It was virtually "heads it will be Matthias, and tails it will be Justus." And interestingly many people believe the wrong choice may have been made, for Matthias, who was chosen, was never heard of again.

That practice, of course, rests back on the Proverb that says:

> The lot is cast into the lap,
> but the decision is wholly from the Lord.[9]

And it is a practice found in many parts of the Scripture. It also finds some expression in our day. Not long ago, the Coptic Church in Ethiopia was to pick a new archbishop, and the choice had been narrowed to six candidates. The delegates put the names in a hat or bowl and took a little child, prayed, and let the child pick a name. That, they believed, was the man to be the archbishop of the Coptic Church.

I can neither condemn nor endorse the practice; it is in the Scripture. The most interesting part of it to me (and it is the part that so startles and contradicts much of the world) is the kind of belief it presupposes. It proclaims flatly that we are not subject to a chance universe, that somehow the sovereignty of God is such that He prevails over the seemingly random circumstances of life. The fact that God can do this is beyond challenge to me, but with the whole of Scripture and history in hand, I'm faced with the question of whether this is God's way for us.

I believe it is not the perfect way.

The New Testament and man's experience since its writing show us God has given His Holy Spirit to lead and

8. Acts 1:15-26
9. Proverbs 16:33

comfort people. He had not done so at the time of the choosing of Matthias nor, of course, at the time of the Old Testament episodes. This makes a big difference. And we see why in St. Paul's description of how the Lord leads His followers[10]:

> . . . what person knows a man's thoughts except the spirit of the man which is in him?

The Spirit knows the mind of God, and He has been given to us that we might know. Pressing this to its logical conclusion, St. Paul was able to observe:

> . . . we have the mind of Christ.

That reveals to us the more perfect way. Resident within us, is the one Person who knows infallibly the will of God: the Holy Spirit, Who was given to the church on the Day of Pentecost nearly 2,000 years ago.

But, you say, how can I distinguish His voice from my own? Jesus explained it this way:

> "My sheep hear My voice, and I know them, and they follow Me . . ."[11]

I have found there is a difference between my voice and that of the Lord. God's voice, when acted upon, brings peace and rest inwardly. I have learned that my own voice when acted upon contrary to the will of the Lord brings exactly the opposite. Experience—trial and error—will prove the distinctiveness of that genuine, still, small voice.

St. Paul gave us the assurance of it, but as he so often did, he laid down some conditions[12]:

---

10. I Corinthians 2:11-16
11. John 10:27
12. Romans 12:1-2

I appeal to you...to present your bodies a living sacrifice, holy and acceptable to God, which is your spiritual worship.

The first thing to do, he said, is to present your whole being—everything—to God, because it is *you,* the living you, He wants, not your *things.* This requires an act of the will, like a sacrifice on the altar, only it is spiritual worship not ritual worship. In fact there is no worship unless this is done. You worship God only by giving yourself to Him. As you do it, you are holy and acceptable because of Jesus Christ.

Then comes step two:

Do not be conformed to this world but be transformed by the renewal of your mind, *that you may prove what is the will of God,* what is good and acceptable and perfect.

The act of giving yourself will transform your mind; you will not think as this present age thinks. Instead, your mind will be conformed to the mind of the Lord by the influence of the Holy Spirit, and you will do His will.

Paul said it even more simply in another letter:

...God is at work in you, both to *will* and to *work* for His good pleasure.[13]

Do you get the picture? God *wants* you to do His will, and He has made it possible, even easy, for you to do it. He cleansed you of your sins by sending His Son Jesus to die for you, and He sent the Holy Spirit into you, planting His own nature *within* you.

All that is required is for you to surrender yourself to Him by an act of your will and come under His sovereignty, where His will is done on earth as it is in heaven. You begin

13. Philippians 2:13

simply by verbalizing it: "Lord, I present myself to you as a living sacrifice without reservation." As you continue to verbalize it daily, the reality of it will become more and more evident in your life. Then it is up to Him to show you what to do and how to do it; the responsibility is His and He fully assumes it with ease. It is no problem for Him. You don't have to worry about *how* He will do it. He has thousands of ways. He knows exactly how to lead you according to His will and purpose; He knows how to make you recognize His voice.

Seek first the kingdom of God, and everything else will come into its rightful place. That is a promise.

*   *   *

Life is something like a road with deep ditches lining the sides. The ditches beckon often. I remember the day a feeling welled up within me, a desire to disrupt my ministry for several weeks to make a unique trip across the European-Asian land mass with some friends. Almost simultaneously rose the feeling that God might not want me to be gone so long. I was nervous about it. That was a red flag; the ditch was beckoning.

The flag told me I was not yielded to the Lord regarding the trip. If I were, He would disincline my heart, and the desire would not be there. If my heart, my inner self, is not at peace, then I am not yielded. But once I literally and verbally surrendered the matter to the Lord, by an act of the will, peace came into my heart, my mind, my inner self. The desire faded, and before long the opportunity for the trip evaporated. God was at work in me both to will and then to do His good pleasure.

Another ditch beckoned when the opportunity came to minister at a place not usually open to renewal. I didn't want to go, even though I felt I probably should. Lack of inner peace popped the red flag up until I took time to reflect and surrender the entire matter to the Lord, asking Him to change my heart if it was His will. He did, and I gradually found myself really wanting to go. Again, He was at work within me to cause me both to will and to do His good pleasure.

In that manner I stay on the road, avoiding ditches, as I am guided by the inner peace that the Holy Spirit is able to give. Turmoil is my red flag.

The cross provides an extreme example. It was a terrible time; the ditches on each side of Christ's road beckoned. And yet He went to the cross.

"Father, if Thou art willing, remove this cup from Me..."

The ditch beckoned. The flesh did not want to do that which He knew His Father wanted.

"...nevertheless not My will, but Thine, be done..."[14]

He yielded. And God's will was done. You see, He did not want the cross; He wanted the fulfillment of His Father's will. That happened to lead to the cross, and He went willingly, with total inner peace.

God changes our wills to conform to His—to the degree that we yield our wills to Him.

* * *

It took me a number of years to reach a proper understanding of two Scripture verses that Jesus wants us to experience as we seek His will for our lives. One says:

For this is the love of God, that we keep His commandments. And *His commandments are not burdensome (grievous).*[15]

14. Luke 22:42
15. I John 5:3

THY WILL BE DONE ON EARTH

I had found some of those commandments to be pretty hard myself. What could this mean?

And then there is this:

> "Take My yoke upon you, and learn from Me; for I am gentle and lowly in heart, and you will find rest for your souls. For *My yoke is easy, and My burden is light*." [16]

Frankly I wasn't too sure about that either. But then experience showed this: If I am yoked with Jesus Christ, His yoke is easy on me only if I'm going in the same direction He's going. If He wants to go to the left, and I want to go to the right, then suddenly the yoke becomes very uncomfortable. If I'm in agreement with the Lord, then His commandments are no longer burdensome. That is the lesson.

So what am I learning? In order to discern the Lord's will about something, I say, "Lord, I don't want to do this unless you want me to. If you want me to do it, incline my heart; if you don't want me to do it, disincline my heart."

Then I talk with my wife, my friends, proven counselors. And, very importantly, I use the brains God gave me. I weigh alternatives. And little by little things begin to happen. I find a solid, reasonable desire that I can trust growing within me to go one or another direction.

I declare this unequivocally: I cannot think of a single time where I honestly sought the Lord to hear His will and trusted Him to incline or disincline my heart, that I failed to come to a decision I believed was the right one. And always I ended up doing what I wanted to do.

Do not misunderstand me. I did what I wanted to do, believing God had governed my heart.

God is not out to trick us. He *wants* us to walk in unity and harmony with His Holy Spirit. That's why our Lord

16. Matthew 11:29-30

Jesus Christ prayed so confidently to His Father, "Thy kingdom come, thy will be done, on earth as it is in heaven."

* * *

There is a disturbing teaching going around the land that should be touched on in any discussion of the will of God. It centers on the thesis that if you somehow pray *hard enough,* if you somehow have *enough faith,* you can get God to do anything. People have been telling the body of Christ that you can go to God and get anything you want, if you ask *in faith.*

I heard a man stand up at a meeting in Dallas and ask the people, "Do you want a Cadillac? Well, go down to the Cadillac store, lay your hands on one and *claim* it. God will give it to you. Try it." That is an extreme example, but I heard it with my own ears.

The teaching is particularly rampant at healing meetings. I've heard ministers ask, "Do you have enough faith?" And they exhort desperately sick people to "have more faith."

One wonders, "How much does it take anyway?" Jesus said if we had faith as a grain of mustard seed we could move mountains,[17] and His point was that faith is not a matter of how much we have. He was repudiating that idea by comparing the required amount with a grain of mustard seed, which is almost indescribably small. The issue, He said, lies in the object of the faith. In what is the faith placed? So many teachers seem to be telling us to have *faith in our faith.* That's heresy. We can't say, "Lord, I've got my faith all built up—I've got a bucketful. Now I demand that you do this. I claim it!" That's all backwards.

God is not a glorified genie in a bottle. Prayer is not tantamount to rubbing Aladdin's lamp to get Him to come out and do our will.

I've run into well-meaning people all over the country

---

17. Matthew 17:20

who have unwittingly developed the idea that prayer is persuading God to do something. They deny it, but they're actually trying to twist the arm of God, thinking subconsciously that if they twist hard enough, they can get Him to do anything. Faith will move mountains, they say. But what if God doesn't want the mountain moved? When Jesus said that if two people agreed about something in prayer it would be granted, it seems obvious that His purpose in calling for such agreement was to guarantee that they would be agreeing on the will of the Lord. If they, under the influence of the Holy Spirit, agreed, then it was likely they had found God's will. It's not a matter of the two of them being able to muster more strength to twist His arm. That would make them God, and God would be the servant.

No, prayer does not move the reluctant arm of God. It is a part of God's plan for accomplishing *His* purpose. He has chosen us to be collaborers, to work together with Him. He can burden our hearts for those things He wants us to pray for, but He will not let us persuade Him against His will.

Now the Lord does sometimes allow us to have things we improperly want—usually for the purpose of instructing us—but we must not abuse the Scripture to get it to say that this is the right way.

We learn this from the recorded lives of the people of Israel. Samuel, for instance, when he became a very old man, was approached by the people with their complaints.[18] "Samuel, we're sick of this. We want to have a king; we want to be like other nations."

Samuel was upset. "No, you are not to be like other nations. God is your King."

But the people insisted, and the Lord yielded. "Samuel, tell them they can have a king, but they will be awfully sorry." He knew the kings would exploit them. Their sons would be pressed into military service, their daughters would be forced into harems, their men and women would be

18. I Samuel 8:4-22

ordered into servanthood. But God let it happen.

The psalmist spoke of such turnabouts in this way:

> . . . He gave them their request; but sent leanness into
> their soul.[19]

To go against the will of God can do nothing but diminish life. Jesus taught His disciples that they were to combat that by never asking God to do anything other than His will and purpose. They were never to seek to impose their wills.

With that well registered in their minds, they were ready to move on—living in the will of God.

---

19. Psalm 106:15 (KJV)

❧ Six ❧

Give Us This Day
Our Daily Bread

ONCE WE HAVE placed God in His superior place—as God—then we can see with far better vision that He really does care about us and cares about us in infinite detail. We have a response to those people who feel that God is concerned only with the great issues of life and cannot be troubled with their day-to-day problems. I've had many tell me they can pray for others but not for themselves. "I just can't imagine He wants me bringing my petty little needs to Him."

That attitude is often rooted in a misunderstanding of this passage of Scripture:

"Do not be like them (the gentiles), for your Father knows what you need before you ask Him."[1]

That appears to be a contradiction to the words, "give us this day our daily bread." If He knows what we need, then why ask Him? Why pray at all?

1. Matthew 6:8

Jacques Ellul of France, a leading Christian thinker, has offered the best answer I know: we make petition and intercession simply because the Lord told us to.

*   *   *

Let's look carefully at this sentence: "Give us this day our daily bread."

It begins with the word "give," a word carefully chosen by Jesus to teach us that the Lord God is the *sole source of supply for everything we need*.

God's way of supply is through means He has provided, and this can be through other people along with our own efforts. But above and beneath and beyond it all must be the awareness and the confidence that *He* is the source. However we don't always live as though we know that. We often look at our employers as the source of our supply, and we panic if we lose our jobs simply because we have been looking so long at the intermediary, thinking of them as the source. The truth is, if we find ourselves out of work, the Lord is simply changing the delivery boy of His blessing.

The same is true in every area of life. Consider healing. We honor medical science and all those who have discovered the ways in which our bodies work, and that's good. Through study and probing, scientists and doctors have been able to understand some of the laws the Lord God has established. They can help bring the body back into harmony with Him when it gets out of sorts. But we must not forget that God puts into the minds of men the ability to unlock the secrets of the world and of our physical bodies. He is the source of all health and healing. As long as that is remembered, He is not dishonored when we turn to doctors.

Sometimes, of course, He works directly, without intermediaries, and extraordinary healings occur. But miracles are not, in my opinion, God's customary way of working, simply because they are not necessary for Him to execute His will. When they are necessary, they occur. Since He is the God of nature, it would suggest there was something wrong with His laws if He were constantly overriding them. And that is not the case. Sometimes, however, we mess up the creation—the natural order—and God then shows that He is not a prisoner of that creation by overriding and moving beyond His own laws. When He does, we have a miracle.

But the point is, no matter how the healing takes place, God is the source. This guarantees we will come to Him with a right perspective. We are the receivers; He is the source of infinite supply.

*   *   *

"Give *us* this day our daily bread." It's interesting that the singular pronoun—I, me, my, mine—appears nowhere in this prayer. It's always plural.

Jesus is saying, "Don't be concerned only for yourself. You share a common humanity."

The disciples were to hear Him make this point more concisely when He said that the fulfillment of the law of God is to love Him with your whole heart and your neighbor as yourself.[2] And they were to come to know the "us" did not include only their wives and children but rather the entire family of God including multitudes who did not have enough bread.

The next two words are significant too: "this day." Jesus said, "Pray and live for this day." That causes me to wince because I find that most of my concerns are for tomorrow. We're a people who seem to be constantly standing on tiptoe peering over the horizon, trying to see what's coming.

This admonition doesn't mean, of course, that we are not to plan for the future. It simply means we are not to be preoccupied with it. A deep concern about the days ahead may diminish the full enjoyment of today's walk with the Lord. With Him, I've found, it is one day at a time.

The tension becomes even greater when we see the day-

2. Matthew 22:37-40

to-day emphasis compounded in the Lord's Prayer. "Give us *this day* our *daily* bread." We're asking Him to give us *no more* than what we need for this day.

We see this principle established in God's early dealings with His chosen people when they wandered in the wilderness, and He taught them in their extremities. The Israelites had been out of Egypt for less than two months when they began to complain about their lack of food, declaring that they would have rather stayed in bondage in Egypt than to die from hunger.[3]

> Then the Lord said to Moses, "Behold, I will rain bread from heaven for you; and the people shall go out and gather *a day's portion* every day, that I may prove them, whether thay will walk in My law or not . . .

That is striking. God was to *prove* them by *providing* for them, one day at a time. His name, as we've seen, is Provider.

> "On the sixth day, when they prepare what they bring in, it will be twice as much as they gather daily." So Moses and Aaron said to all the people of Israel, "At evening you shall know that it was the Lord who brought you out of the land of Egypt, and in the morning you shall see the glory of the Lord, because He has heard your murmurings against the Lord."

Then we see the fulfillment:

> In the evening quails came up and covered the camp; and in the morning dew lay round about the camp.

I learned something about those birds during many months in the Sinai that illustrates the profound workings of God

---

3. Exodus 16

by very ordinary means. In the winter the birds from Central
Europe migrate to the southern parts of Africa. They pass
over the Sinai and, in each direction, use it as a resting
place. Exhausted, they simply drop down and rest, virtually
unable to move, and then they fly on. It happens twice a
year, and that apparently is what happened with the quail
in the Exodus episode. God didn't even have to disrupt the
natural order with a miracle to accomplish this seemingly
miraculous provision for His people. All they had to do was
pick the quail off the ground in numbers we couldn't believe.

And then there was the morning blessing:

> ... when the dew had gone up, there was on the face
> of the wilderness a fine, flake-like thing, fine as hoar-
> frost on the ground. When the people of Israel saw
> it, they said to one another, "What is it?" For they
> did not know what it was.

In Hebrew, the question "What is it?" is two words,
"man hu," which is rendered "manna." Never having seen
the thing before, they called it, "What is it?"

> And Moses said to them, "It is the bread which the
> Lord has given you to eat. This is what the Lord has
> commanded: 'Gather of it, every man of you, as much
> as he can eat; you shall take an omer apiece, according
> to the number of persons whom each of you has in
> his tent.'" And the people of Israel did so ... And
> Moses said to them, "Let no man leave any of it till
> the morning." But they did not listen to Moses; some
> left part of it till the morning; and it bred worms and
> became foul; and Moses was angry with them. Morn-
> ing by morning they gathered it, each as much as he
> could eat; but when the sun grew hot, it melted.
> On the sixth day they gathered twice as much bread,
> two omers apiece; and when all the leaders of the
> congregation came and told Moses, he said to them,
> "This is what the Lord has commanded: 'Tomorrow

is a day of solemn rest, a holy sabbath to the Lord; bake what you will bake and boil what you will boil, and all that ıs left over lay by to be kept till the morning.'" So they laid it by till the morning, as Moses bade them; and it did not become foul, and there were no worms in it. Moses said, "Eat it today, for today is a sabbath to the Lord; today you will not find it in the field."

God's provision for the children of Israel, from whom we are supposed to learn, was a daily one. Being just like us, they thought of the very thing we 20th century people would think of. Why not go out on Monday, work a little longer and gather enough for the whole week? Why get up so early *every* morning? Well, that wouldn't work. The "thing" melted when the sun got up in the sky. They needed more time to learn.

You can almost hear them thinking just the way we would. "I'll get up before dawn and work really hard and fast. I'll go all out and collect enough 'what is it?' to last the family the whole week." They tried it, rushing back and forth and scooping the stuff up as fast as they could, storing it in their tents. Then they breathed easy, eating well that day.

But the next morning, rubbing their empty stomachs, they went to their supply. It was filled with worms.

God would not let them have more than one day's supply on hand except to accommodate the sabbath. He would not let their enterprise blunt their awareness of His concern for them. This causes one to reflect, first on the huge, well-stocked supermarkets around our land, many open around the clock daily, and, second on our generally dulled perception of the presence of the Lord. There obviously is a relationship.

God taught His people that they were constantly dependent upon Him. It's easy to imagine a child talking to his mother at night. "What are we going to eat tomorrow, Mom? There's nothing in the cupboard."

"I know, child, but God will supply. He has taught us to turn to Him every day, one day at a time. He is faithful to us."

"Yes, Mom, but can't we ever get a little ahead? We ought to plan ahead. What happens if He doesn't supply some day?"

"Oh, but child, that can't happen. He is the source of continual supply. All the time. One day at a time."

It saddens me to imagine what such a conversation would be like in most parts of our affluent society today. Is it any wonder that the people who don't have many possessions often seem to have a keener, more durable faith than those who have enough and are well hedged for the future?

That is why the Lord took the children of Israel right to the edge of hunger day after day. They were learning to say, "Give us this day our daily bread."

*   *   *

The Greek word *epiousios,* from which we translate "daily" in the Lord's Prayer, is not found anywhere in Greek literature. This perplexed Bible scholars for years, even as early as the second century. Many thought Matthew had made it up. But when the Dead Sea Scrolls were found in 1947, these ancient Biblical manuscripts contained many discoveries. Among them was a little fragment of papyrus on which was scratched, of all things, a shopping list, apparently a housewife's notes of things to buy. On that list was the word *epiousios.* What did it mean?

It turned out to be a *category,* items to be purchased *daily.* Some things—grain, oil, salt—could be purchased in quantities and kept for use as needed, but since there was no refrigeration then, such items as milk, fresh fruit and meat had to be purchased each day. That was the word the Holy Spirit inspired the writers to use in their Greek rendering of the Lord's words. He was teaching the disciples that Almighty God was deeply concerned about the little, ordinary needs of everyday life.

Christ's use of the word "bread" shows us something, too. Semanticists and others who work with words and grammar would say He used a synecdoche, a figure of speech "by which a part is put for the whole." More simply, He used one word to stand for a number of things. He didn't mean only something made out of flour, salt and water; He used "bread" to stand for everything needed for the sustenance of life.

We see this in the Lord's provision for the children of Israel, for in addition to food, of course, they needed water. When they camped at Rephidim in the wilderness, there was no water to drink, and once again they were fearful and began to turn against their leader, Moses.

> And the Lord said to Moses, "Pass on before the people, taking with you some of the elders of Israel; and take in your hand the rod with which you struck the Nile, and go. Behold, I will stand before you there on the rock at Horeb; and you shall strike the rock, and water shall come out of it, that the people may drink." And Moses did so, in the sight of the elders of Israel. And he called the name of that place Massah and Meribah, because of the faultfinding of the children of Israel, and because they put the Lord to the proof by saying, "Is the Lord among us or not?"[4]

They, like us, had begun to doubt the Lord's presence when they found themselves in a situation of need. They somehow thought, as we do centuries later, that if God is with you, you can't have any needs, which is not true. God allows us to have needs so we might learn of His infinite supply, but He never leaves us.

When I was a little child, I loved magnets. I was absolutely fascinated by the fact that I could pour filings onto a flat glass surface, like a glass tabletop, move the magnet

---

4. Exodus 17:5-7

all around on the underside of the glass, and the iron filings would march around according to where I put the magnet. I still find that mysterious. The little bits of iron simply follow the magnet, unfailingly.

This is exactly what happened to the children of Israel. They moved, and the Lord was with them. As St. Paul teaches us:

> . . . they drank from the supernatural Rock which followed them, and the Rock was Christ.[5]

He was always there, meeting their every need. We Christians today need to grasp this. We don't even have to invoke His presence; He is there.

> ". . . I am with you always, to the close of the age."[6]

We recognize this when we ask the Lord God to give us this day our daily bread, intimating that we depend upon Him for every single need of life, every day.

*   *   *

This leads us to an understanding of the day-to-day walk that Jesus wants to give us. It is best described near the end of the chapter containing the Lord's Prayer in St. Matthew's gospel, a passage well known but little absorbed in the inner being of most of us:[7]

> "Therefore I tell you, do not be anxious about your life, what you shall eat or what you shall drink, nor about your body, what you shall put on. Is not life more than food, and the body more than clothing? . . ."

5. I Corinthians 10:4
6. Matthew 28:20
7. Matthew 6:25-34

The counsel of the Lord is: don't be anxious. Don't say, as the children of Israel did, "Is the Lord among us?" Don't "murmur" as they did in the wilderness—which God has a name for: Massah and Meribah. The words mean "proof" and "contention," names given "because of the faultfinding of the children of Israel," and because they kept demanding proof from the Lord. Jesus is saying, "Don't be that way. Don't force the Father to say, 'Massah and Meribah.'"

"... Look at the birds of the air: they neither sow nor reap nor gather into barns, and yet your heavenly Father feeds them. Are you not of more value than they? And which of you by being anxious can add one cubit to his span of life?..."

We need to see the futility of anxiety; anxiety is tantamount to finding fault with God, and it is also useless.

"... And why are you anxious about clothing? Consider the lilies of the field, how they grow; they neither toil nor spin; yet I tell you, even Solomon in all his glory was not arrayed like one of these. But if God so clothes the grass of the field, which today is alive and tomorrow is thrown into the oven, will He not much more clothe you, O men of little faith? Therefore do not be anxious, saying, 'What shall we eat?' or 'What shall we drink?' or 'What shall we wear?' For the Gentiles seek all these things..."

Gentiles here are those who are not the people of God but of the world. "Don't act like everyone else," He said, and then delivered one of the most significant instructions of the Scripture which we've mentioned briefly but which should be read again and again:

"... seek first His kingdom and His righteousness, and all these things shall be yours as well."

The priority is clear. It is the theme of the entire Lord's Prayer. The things of God must come first, and then everything else will fall into place.

"Seek first His kingdom." What is His kingdom? It is that place where His will is done. Seek to live there and all your daily needs, everything you need for your sustenance, will be supplied. There will be no anxiety, no worry, no strain.

And then He completed the circle, turning to the day-by-day theme:

> "Therefore do not be anxious about tomorrow, for tomorrow will be anxious for itself. Let the day's own trouble be sufficient for the day."

God deals daily—one step at a time—in our growth into ultimate perfection. We must live daily, not in worry, but in quiet trust. He who is the Rock that follows us each day has the inexhaustible supply for our needs.

❧ Seven ❧

And Forgive Us Our Debts as We Also Have Forgiven Our Debtors

EMBEDDED PROMINENTLY IN Jesus's outline for prayer and life is the doctrine standing at the center of the Christian faith from the beginning—the forgiveness of sins. If you want to live in the will of God, He said, you will regularly include in your prayers a concern for your debts, your trespasses, your sins.

But our grasp of this cardinal teaching is not always as thorough as it should be. For it is a truth that touches the life of the Christian every day, since there is never a time when we do not stand in need of God's forgiveness in some way. Transcending that frightening fact, however, is the certainty that there is something we can do about those things—each day—when we have failed the Lord God. And that is what Jesus wants us to remember.

Some factors in everyone's life and in his or her relationship to God are not always as they should be; yet with many, the awareness doesn't get more precise than that. They simply don't acknowledge that they need much forgiveness.

I suspect a majority of people, including many Christians, think of themselves as relatively decent people leading well-ordered lives that allow them to say, "Oh, there may be a little thing or two—you know, petty things—but basically I lead a pretty good life." They find it offensive to use the words of the great confession in the Book of Common Prayer which teaches us to think of ourselves as "miserable offenders." People often pray that prayer with a condescending tolerance that allows them to think inwardly, "Well, I'm praying this along with those people who really need it."

Unhappily the temperament of our day—the attitude pounded into us by so much of our literature, our television programming, our educational systems—is that *compared with others* we are not such miserable offenders at all. We can always find others with whom we can stand as paragons of virtue. That's our downfall. We measure ourselves against one another, and it's easy to slip into a mentality that says, "Compared with that terrible drunkard, Joe, I'm a pretty good person."

When Jesus talked about forgiveness, however, He didn't allow this. He set a very high standard:

"You, therefore, must be perfect, as your heavenly Father is perfect."[1]

I do not measure up to that standard. I'm far more comfortable when thinking of myself in terms of other people. But the Lord said I couldn't do that. He told me to stop seeing myself in terms of the rest of the people in my acquaintance and to see myself the way God sees me. That terrifies me, of course, for my tendency is to believe that if people really knew me as I am, they wouldn't like me. But that's not the way it is with God. He wants me perfect but sees me the way I am and still loves me, granting me grace upon grace to live and to grow to the point where I will be perfect.

1. Matthew 5:48

"Forgive us our sins," He said, knowing the true character of the Father.

*   *   *

Many people, often subconsciously, think of God as a kind of indulgent grandfather, slightly senile, off in the heavens somewhere, sentimental and mushy, benignly watching over His children, happy to pat us on the head and overlook our indiscretions. That picture, however, is not found on the pages of Holy Scripture. The God we meet in the Bible is One whose most distinguishing characteristic is absolute and total holiness. He's powerful, certainly, but that's not the overriding characteristic. The Bible says He is holy above all; the host of heaven sings before Him:

"Holy, holy, holy, is the Lord God Almighty, Who was and is and is to come!"[2]

He dwells in inaccessible light, the Scripture says; in Him is no shadow of turning, no variation or shadow due to change.[3] He has no dark thoughts, being fully transparent; there are no secret feelings of hatred and resentment. He is love throughout—love cast in total holiness.

That is hard for us to absorb, but it is why He cannot and will not tolerate evil.

One of the most moving visions presented in Scripture is a vision given to Isaiah before he began his prophetic ministry. It casts in bright light the dynamic behind the truth of forgiveness.[4]

In the year that King Uzziah died I saw the Lord sitting upon a throne, high and lifted up; and His train filled the temple. Above Him stood the seraphim; each had

2. Revelation 4:8
3. James 1:17
4. Isaiah 6:1-7

six wings: with two he covered his face, and with two he covered his feet, and with two he flew. And one called to another and said:

"Holy, holy, holy is the Lord of hosts;
the whole earth is full of His glory."

And the foundations of the thresholds shook at the voice of him who called, and the house was filled with smoke.

If you close your eyes tightly, you can almost see it with Isaiah. He saw a magnificent vision of the Lord God—and it was only a vision, for no one has ever seen God[5]—entering a moment of true worship as he felt himself taken into the presence of the Almighty. Notice his first perception of himself as he envisioned the Lord, high and lifted up:

And I said: "Woe is me! For I am lost; for I am a man of unclean lips, and I dwell in the midst of a people of unclean lips; for my eyes have seen the King, the Lord of hosts!"

Isaiah's first thought upon seeing this magnificent vision of the holy God was his own unworthiness.

Reflect on it a moment. I've had people come and say, "I just don't understand this matter of sin. I don't feel like a sinner." I know one of two things is at the heart of the matter. One, they have an understanding that links sin to punishable crime, like murder or bank robbery; and most of them are not guilty of such charges. They have failed to see sin as *any* violation of the will and purpose of God. Or two, they have never been aware of standing in the presence of the holy God. If they had, they would have had the same reaction as Isaiah. I know from personal experience that they would have also cried, "Woe is me!"

Note that Isaiah's first reaction was his awareness of his

---

5. John 1:18

unclean *lips*. That is a perfect expression of sinfulness, as Jesus explained when He declared:

> "...what comes out of the mouth proceeds from the heart..."[6]

The things we say are a reflection of our deep being, and Isaiah perceived his unclean lips as an indicator of his unclean heart. He felt a *personal* guilt in the sight of the holy God, and he also recognized the *corporate* guilt of his people. He *knew* the need for forgiveness.

And he immediately acknowledged his guilt. Such acknowledgment was implied in Jesus' words when He told the disciples to say, "Forgive us our debts." To pray that way is to declare, "I am guilty." It rejects the way of Adam, who, when confronted by God after eating the forbidden fruit in the Garden of Eden, blurted out, "The woman *You* gave me; she made me do it."

Think of that answer. Not only did Adam try to shift the blame to his wife, but also to God Himself. "It really is *Your* fault, Lord, because You gave her to me."

Eve was no better. When God spoke to her, she said, "The devil made me do it," using a line of buck-passing heard in many Christian circles today.

Not so with Isaiah. "I'm guilty," he declared.

Fortunately, that was not the end of his experience, and we must see that. For many people come to a knowledge of their sin and then are plunged into such despair that they never recover. That is not God's plan.

> Then flew one of the seraphim to me, having in his hand a burning coal which he had taken with tongs from the altar. And he touched my mouth, and said: "Behold, this has touched your lips; your guilt is taken away, and your sin forgiven."[7]

---

6. Matthew 15:18
7. Isaiah 6:6-7

Immediately Isaiah moved from a deep sense of sinfulness in the sight of God to one of cleansing and forgiveness. The altar is a symbol of the presence of God. Thus healing, forgiveness and cleansing were carried to him *from God,* for Isaiah did not in his vision go to the altar; rather God reached out, as it were, cleansing and purifying him, right where he was.

The pattern is important: first, the vision of the holy God; immediately the awareness of the sinful self; then the cleansing and forgiveness. It opens up a crucial point. For if God were only holy and righteous, we would be in hopeless trouble. But, in a mystery too deep for human penetration, God is at the same time and always a loving and merciful God.

Now this fact, in a sense, left God with a problem regarding His creation from the very beginning. He knew that, in fashioning man with the ability to choose, He was bringing forth a species that would defy Him. One wonders why He did it. Why not make man incapable of sinning? The only real answer is that He thought it was worth the effort; the problem of sin and its pain were the price of freedom. So He began what looks like a dangerous experiment: He created man in His image, knowing full well what would happen. But let there be no misunderstanding. He handled the matter of man's defection even before the creation. That is why Jesus is spoken of as "the Lamb slain from the foundation of the world."[8] We must never think God was caught by surprise and had to improvise to rescue a world fallen away. He knew the cost of what He was doing, and paid it.

Isaiah had a glimpse of that. "Forgive us our sins..."

* * *

To enlarge our own vision, we need to see the completeness of what God has done to overcome man's offense

---

8. Revelation 13:8 (KJV)

against the standard of holiness. The Scripture instructs us through Moses and the establishment of the day of atonement, Yom Kippur.[9]

First, God told Aaron the high priest to atone for his own sin with the offering of a ram.

> "Then he shall take . . . two goats, and set them before the Lord at the door of the tent of meeting; and Aaron shall cast lots upon the two goats, one lot for the Lord and the other lot for Azazel."

Now the Bible makes clear that the blood of rams and goats cannot atone for a single sin. In Aaron's case, they were merely part of the preparation of Israel for the principle of atonement. One would indeed come, the Lamb of God, whose death on a cross would atone for the sins of the whole earth. In faith and obedience, from the heart, the children of Israel "drew" as it were upon Christ's one redeeming sacrifice.

The first goat was killed and offered in sacrifice. There is something we need to learn from the example of the second goat:

> ". . . Aaron shall lay both his hands upon the head of the live goat, and confess over him all the iniquities of the people of Israel, and all their transgressions, all their sins; and he shall put them upon the head of the goat, and send him away into the wilderness . . . The goat shall bear all their iniquities upon him to a solitary land . . ."

Imagine that you are a Jew witnessing this ritual on the day of atonement. There are two goats. One is slain to remind you that the innocent was to die for the guilty, but one is presented alive. All the sins of you and your people are confessed openly and cast upon the head of the goat.

9. Leviticus 16:5-22

Then he is released, sent away. Your eyes, and all in Israel, are focused on that goat as he makes his way out of the camp and over the wasteland. You watch as he gets smaller and smaller in the distance. Finally he disappears and is gone forever—with your sins.

The Lord wants us to fathom in our deepest recesses that not only is our sin forgiven, but it is also borne away. The guilt is taken away, totally. As with the scapegoat, the one let loose, it is gone—out of sight, out of mind.

Jesus would have us remember that.

We leap into the New Testament and find St. Paul carrying us even further in our understanding:[10]

> Therefore, if any one is in Christ, he is a new creation;
> the old has passed away, behold, the new has come.
> All this is from God . . .

It was God's idea. He did it. Flesh and blood couldn't accomplish such a transformation.

> . . . who through Christ reconciled us to Himself . . .

We must see that man and God are out of harmony. We don't understand man's condition until we realize there is estrangement, separation. But St. Paul tells us God has done something about it. He has reconciled us to Himself. What does that mean?

> . . . that is, God was in Christ reconciling the world to Himself, *not counting their trespasses against them.* . . .

It is done. As far as God is concerned, the reconciliation has occurred. He has taken our sins and placed them on the head of Jesus Christ who became the Sin Bearer as well as

---

10. II Corinthians 5:17-20

the Lamb of God, whose death upon the cross actually did atone for the sins of the entire earth.

However, reconciliation is a two-way street. It will not do for one party in an estrangement to be reconciled if the other is not. If a husband is out of sorts with his wife and wants to make up, there can be no reconciliation until the wife wants it, too. So, Paul said, we must do something about it:

> . . . We beseech you on behalf of Christ, *be reconciled to God.*

There is the cruncher. God did something to solve the sin problem. He did it through Christ as an objective fact. What remains is for people to be reconciled to Him. He's done His part. They can live their entire lives in hostility to Him and His will—in unreconciliation—if they choose. And many choose to do so. But that does not change the fact that He has solved the problem from His side.

That's what the Scripture means when it speaks of proclaiming the gospel, which means "good news," for it is good news to learn that everything necessary to dispose of man's sin has been accomplished. All man has to do is receive it and live in it.

That's what Jesus wants us to recall when we pray, "Forgive us our debts."

*   *   *

In the New Testament, five Greek words are used to speak of sin, each with a slightly different overtone. When we pray the Lord's Prayer, we should hear all of those overtones. And although Scripture often interchanges the words to provide various emphases, we should be familiar with their basic meanings.

One of the words is *hamartia*. It means "missing the mark." Imagine you are shooting an arrow at a target and it falls short; it fails to reach its objective. That is *hamartia*.

It is the sin of failing to be what God wants you to be, failing to be what you might have been. To fail to be the husband or wife or parent you should be is *hamartia*. Those using the Book of Common Prayer recall this when they say:

> . . . we confess that we have sinned against Thee
> in thought, word, and deed,
> by what we have done,
> and *by what we have left undone*.

The second word is *parabasis*. It means "stepping across the line"—trespassing—and is deliberate disobedience. Think of the sign "no trespassing." It means "keep off." When you step across the line into the place where you have no business being, you have committed *parabasis*. There is nothing accidental about it.

A third word is *paraptoma*, which involves "slipping across." It is not an intentional, premeditated act. The difference between it and parabasis is a bit like the distinction between manslaughter and murder. Motive is the key. *Paraptoma* might well describe the man walking on a patch of ice, falling down and hurting himself. He should not have been on the ice in the first place.

Then there is *anomia*, an altogether different category. The word means "without law" and is often translated "lawlessness." A common word for sin in the New Testament, it centers on attitude and the disposition of the heart. We see it manifest in the desire to "do our own thing," to be a law unto ourselves, to throw off all restraints of family, society, government and God. Outwardly we may appear to be righteous, but inwardly, where it counts with God, there is no righteousness. Often the only thing that keeps us from running wild is the fear of getting caught.

The last word is *opheilema*, which is the one used in the Lord's Prayer and is usually translated "debt." This, of course, means "something owed," and if we reflect on that honestly, we may find ourselves wincing, for it speaks of the things we owe to God or to someone else. We frequently fail to render to God and others what is properly theirs. When we withhold honor from our parents, for example, we have sinned in the sight of God, for the Scripture tells us honor is due them.[11] When we fail to praise God, we sin, for we are told praise is due Him.[12] The same holds true with obedience[13] and loving our neighbor.[14]

Can we then, considering the breadth of our sins, do anything short of following the instructions of Jesus and beg for forgiveness by our Father?

*   *   *

But we can't stop there. The fifth petition of the Lord's Prayer has a condition:

"And forgive us our debts,
As we also have forgiven our debtors."

And that condition is startling; how often I wish it weren't there! But it is, and it's reinforced two verses later:

"For if you forgive men their trespasses, your heavenly Father will also forgive you; but if you do not forgive men their trespasses, neither will your Father forgive your trespasses."

There is a clear connection between our vertical relationship with God and our horizontal relationship with people. The Lord said, in fact, that we cannot have forgiveness beyond our willingness to forgive others. You can almost hear His firm gentleness, "This is the way you should pray, but remember, you are setting a limit to the forgiveness you

---

11. Matthew 15:4
12. Psalm 113:1-3
13. Hebrews 5:9
14. Matthew 22:39

can receive, because you are saying, 'Father, forgive my sins *only* to the extent I am willing to forgive those who have sinned against me."

I have counseled many people, and one of the most prevalent problems everywhere is depression, often very deep. I have become convinced that a central cause is bitterness and resentment in the heart, an unforgiving attitude. It can have deep and wide repercussions that spread outward with strange behavioral and physical manifestations, for forgiveness touches all of life, reflecting our relationship with our Creator and our fellow creatures.

Consequently Jesus allowed no room to ask, "Do those who've offended me deserve forgiveness?" That is irrelevant. He said in effect, "You must be willing to grant forgiveness in order to receive forgiveness."

Peter, being like us, approached Jesus and asked:

"Lord, how often shall my brother sin against me, and I forgive him? As many as seven times?"[15]

He wanted the Lord to tell him when he could say, "Enough is enough!" But Jesus replied:

"I do not say to you seven times, but seventy times seven."

And we certainly cannot take that to mean that on the 491st offense, we are free to punch the offender in the nose. That was simply Jesus' way of saying, "There is no limit to how often you are to forgive a person." He pressed forward with a powerful parable[16] that told of a king who, settling accounts with his servants, forgave one who owed him 10,000 talents—for a laborer, about 15 years' wages. But that servant, who had begged on his knees that the debt be forgiven, went out and immediately encountered a fellow

15. Matthew 18:21-22
16. Matthew 18:23-35

servant who owed him a hundred denarii, a relatively small amount. He demanded payment and when the fellow couldn't do it had him thrown into prison.

> "When his fellow servants saw what had taken place, they were greatly distressed, and they went and reported to their lord all that had taken place. Then his lord summoned him and said to him, 'You wicked servant! I forgave you all that debt because you besought me; and should not you have had mercy on your fellow servant, as I had mercy on you?' And in anger his lord delivered him to the jailers, till he should pay all his debt. *So also my heavenly Father will do to every one of you, if you do not forgive your brother from your heart.*"

This command is hard for many to handle. But St. John gives us some guidelines.[17]
First, he says God is light and then explains that,

> . . . if we walk in the light, as He is in the light, we have fellowship with one another, and the blood of Jesus His Son cleanses us from all sin.

Here is a condition to our being forgiven. We have to walk in the light, having drawn close to the One who is light Himself, and as we do so we are forgiven and cleansed of our sins. But note that it says we simultaneously "have fellowship with one another." Obviously we can't have fellowship—which means to hold things in common—with someone we have a grudge against. What happens is that as we walk in the light—walk with the Lord—we forgive every trespass committed against us, and we are forgiven every trespass we have committed. It cuts both ways.

St. John then issues this warning:

---

17. I John 1:5-7

He who says he is in the light and hates his brother is in the darkness still. [18]

If you hate your brother, not having forgiven him everything he might have done to offend you, you are in the darkness, which means you have turned away from the light, who is God.

Have you ever wondered why so many of the great saints of the church spent so much time speaking and writing about their sinfulness? St. John gives us the reason: the closer one lives to God—in communion with Light—the more one sees his own need for forgiveness. And the more he sees his own need, the more he is ready to forgive others.

Those great saints also knew that the Scriptures teach us three things about our sins after they've been confessed: first, the Lord will take our sins and cast them behind His back. [19] Second, He will separate us from them as far as the east is from the west. [20] And, third, He will remember them no more. [21]

Do you live as though these promises are true? Or do you say something like, "O Lord, here I come again; I mean, You must be pretty tired of this sin by now," and then confess the same old thing over and over?

If His promises are true, then God must reply something like this: "What is this you're talking about? I put that sin out of My mind the first time you confessed it. I remember it no more."

The Scriptures tell us that the continual bringing up of a confessed sin is not a work of the Holy Spirit; it is a work of the evil one, the one known as the accuser of the brethren. [22] He likes to remind God's people of their forgiven sins; it

18. I John 2:9
19. Isaiah 38:17
20. Psalm 103:12
21. Jeremiah 31:34
22. Revelation 12:10

keeps them from moving forward, from maturing. God never does that.

So Jesus said that, when we pray, we should say, "Forgive us our sins..."

My understanding of this, although still imperfect, has revolutionized my life, persuading me to live with an attitude of openness before all Christians. And I say *attitude* only because it is not always appropriate to blurt out everything about yourself to all people all the time. They can get tired of it. But there should be a *willingness* to reveal everything—an attitude of openness, of transparency. This is part of living in the will of God.

⍟ Eight ⍟

And Lead Us Not into Temptation, but Deliver Us from Evil

WE NOW COMPLETE the cycle. Having seen that Jesus wants us to bring Him our present—"give us this day our daily bread"—and our past—"forgive us our debts"—we look at the future:

> And lead us not into temptation,
>   But deliver us from evil.

When we talk about our daily bread our focus is on God the Father who is the Creator and Provider of all we need, and when we speak of forgiveness our attention turns to Jesus the Son, who is our Redeemer. Finally, when we say, "Lead us not into temptation," we look to God the Holy Spirit, the One who guides us through life.

Thus Jesus was telling us to bring the whole of our lives—past, present and future—before the whole of the Godhead: Father, Son, and Holy Spirit. Wholeness and fullness: that was His theme. If you would pray and live wholly and fully, He said, then do this.

What is it we are asking of God when we pray, "Lead us not into temptation"? Why would He want to lead us *into* temptation?

Look at St. Matthew's opening line describing the so-called temptation of Jesus:

> Then Jesus was *led up by the Spirit* into the wilderness to be tempted by the devil.[1]

The verse is unequivocal. Jesus was *led* by God the Holy Spirit to a place for the express purpose of being tempted by the *evil one,* which is a better translation than simply *evil* as found in the Lord's Prayer. And yet He Himself said we should pray, "Lead us *not* into temptation." How are we to understand that apparent contradiction?

This is a problem for students of the Bible, but I believe there is a right way to understand this petition that can clear away the confusion. Look at this instruction from James:

> Count it all joy, my brethren, when you meet various trials . . .[2]

The King James Version of the Bible speaks of "temptations," which is also an accepted rendering of the Greek. In fact, J. B. Phillips used both words in his paraphrase:

> When all kinds of trials and temptations crowd into your lives, my brothers, don't resent them as intruders, but welcome them as friends![3]

James understood something here that eludes many of us. Be happy, he said, in troubles, difficulties and adversity. He knew that when a person makes it his intention to live by the will of God and under the power of the Holy Spirit,

---

1. Matthew 4:1
2. James 1:2
3. The New Testament in Modern English, translated by J. B. Phillips.

---

he will have trials and temptations. He can pray until his knees are numb, asking that he not enter the place of temptation and that he be removed from all difficulties, and that prayer will not be answered.

Most of us would like it to be otherwise. "We'd like to arrange it so that at the moment one becomes a Christian, troubles vanish forever. Think of the converts we'd win, we argue.

But God sees it differently. He does not exempt Christians from the trials of life; neither does He exempt them from temptations. Quite the contrary, life with Him seems to add a few.

What we need, then, is God's way of viewing them; we need to see His purpose. James helps our perception of God's way:

> Let no one say when he is tempted, "I am tempted by God"; for God cannot be tempted with evil and *He Himself tempts no one* . . .[4]

We should be clear on this. We are not to say that God is tempting us, in the sense that He is seeking to lead us away from Himself or that He is putting stumbling blocks in our path to trip us. God does not tempt men to evil.

Jesus was led by the Spirit to the place of temptation, but it was Satan who did the tempting.

What can we say, then? God does not tempt, but He allows us to move into the place of temptation; He will even lead us there. And James said, "Count it all joy when He does that, brethren."

> . . . for you know that the testing of your faith produces steadfastness. And let steadfastness have its full effect, that you may be perfect and complete, lacking in nothing.[5]

---

4. James 1:13
5. James 1:3-4

It becomes clear. God has a purpose in allowing us to be tempted and tested. It can be His will for us to have difficulty.

We tend to see temptation as a test of will power. God sees it as a test of faith, producing in us qualities that will enable us to stand under pressures, to hold fast and firm in the midst of the difficulties of life. God's purpose is to strengthen His people, to mold and fashion their lives to produce maturity. The only way to maturity in Christ is to encounter and overcome difficulties, troubles, trials and, yes, even temptations. It is God's way.

Therefore, He will not remove temptation from your path. He will not remove trials. To do so would be harmful to you. So we must stop looking at troubles from Satan's perspective, because it is clear he would have us move into sin and rebellion against God through discouragement and despair as we lose sight of Who truly governs the universe. Instead, we must look at difficulties from their Godward side, understanding that our Father's intention is to test our faith so as to produce maturity and perfection.

*   *   *

Remember, the prayer is "Lead us not *into* temptation . . ." We need to see what we are asking God to do and not to do, and St. Paul helps us:

No temptation has overtaken you that is not common to man.[6]

What a relief that is! I could not imagine that other people's temptations were like mine; I had assumed no one suffered the same way I did. That's helpful. And St. Paul helps us even more in the very next sentence:

God is faithful . . .

6. I Corinthians 10:13

That is critically important. Remember what James said? "Be joyful when you encounter trials and temptations, for you know that *the testing of your faith* produces steadfastness." What is this faith *in?* That's the issue: not how much you have. If it is in God, then God is faithful. We can depend on His faithfulness. It is that trust which is being built when we are taken to the place of temptation and trial. God is testing—and building—our faith in His faithfulness.

But Paul gives us even more encouragement:

> . . . He will not let you be tempted beyond your strength, but with the temptation will also provide the way of escape, that you may be able to endure it.

Who regulates the severity of temptation? It is clearly God. Not Satan. It's as though God says, "Temptation can go this far and no farther. *I* will not permit it."

Unhappily, many Christians are mixed up on this. If you go into an average Christian bookstore today, you will find almost as many books on the power of Satan as on the power of God. And when you hear people testifying about their spiritual lives, they often talk endlessly about Satan doing this and Satan doing that—"ol' slewfoot really messed me up on that," and so on. I often wonder, "Where is the power of God in all of this?" We would do well to ask, "Why did He come?" and then look at this answer by St. John:

> The reason the Son of God appeared was to destroy the works of the devil.[7]

A central doctrine of the church is that Jesus, who is God, came in the flesh to earth. We celebrate the fact every Christmas.

In Hebrews we learn that Jesus came in the flesh

---

7. I John 3:8

that through death He might *destroy* him who has the power of death, that is, the devil, and *deliver* all those who through fear of death were subject to lifelong bondage.[8]

The Lord took human form to destroy the devil. Did He fail?

No, Jesus did not fail. Satan is a defeated foe, and he knows it. A popular book was entitled *Satan Is Alive and Well on Planet Earth,* and I disagree with the title. Satan *is* alive, but he is not *well.* He is mortally wounded and knows it, but of course he is a liar and a deceiver and the last thing he wants anyone to believe is that he has been defeated by the Lord Jesus Christ. Satan goes to great lengths to convince people that he has invincible power. But that's not true. His power was broken.

Many of us become confused, however, and ask questions like, "If he's defeated, how come I feel his power at work so intensely in my life?" The answer is that God can and will use even Satan to effect His purpose—to perfect His people and bring forth His Kingdom. He will even use the wrath of man to praise Him[9]; that doesn't mean the wrath of man is good, and neither is Satan. It simply means that God is sovereign throughout this universe and can use anything He desires to accomplish His purpose. That purpose is to bring us to maturity.

In the meantime, we faithfully pray, "Lead us not into temptation, but deliver us from evil."

To understand the power of Satan in the lives of Christians, imagine a stake driven into the ground. Tethered on a long chain attached to the stake is a roaring, ravenous lion. As a Christian passes by, the lion sees him, roars and makes a mighty lunge toward him, but he's stopped by the chain and that's as far as he can go. All he can do is roar. However, because of free will, the Christian can, if he wants

8. Hebrews 2:14-15
9. Psalm 76:10

to, walk within the radius of the chain. But he will be consumed, for in that case he is no match for the evil one. However, the lion can't force the Christian to walk within his range. And neither will God lead him within that circle of genuine danger; He will merely let the Christian be tested.

God has set limits on Satan's power. Satan cannot lead us into rebellion and sin unless we agree to cooperate. Remember, Jesus said:

> "All authority (power) in heaven and on earth has been given to me."[10]

That doesn't leave any real authority and power for Satan.

Scripture tells us that Christians have been taken out of the kingdom of darkness over which Satan rules and transferred into the kingdom of God's beloved Son.[11] It's as though we have emblazoned on our foreheads the words "Under New Management." Satan no longer has rights over us unless we give them to him.

Jesus did not fail. The great hymns of the church celebrate only triumph, the victory of Jesus over Satan, death and sin. The Lord Himself spoke of it the night before He died when He prayed:

> "Father . . . glorify Thy Son that the Son may glorify Thee, since Thou hast given Him power over all flesh . . . I glorified Thee on earth, *having accomplished the work which Thou gavest Me to do . . .*"[12]

A few hours later on the cross, He cried out:

> "It is finished."[13]

10. Matthew 28:18
11. Colossians 1:13
12. John 17:1-4
13. John 19:30

That was not a cry of defeat: it was a cry of victory. He has delivered us from the evil one and continues to do so day by day.

Scripture shows us God has always used the trial-and-temptation method of testing and teaching His people, even before Calvary. Then as now, Satan was not able to do just anything he wanted.

This is a lesson of the book of Job, which scholars tell us was the first portion of the Bible written. The first chapter opens with God throwing a big party which was attended, seemingly, by everybody who was anybody, including Satan. How he got there, we don't know.

We see the Lord God indulging in a bit of boasting with Satan: "Have you noticed my servant Job, how upright and righteous he is?"

Satan replies, "It's not surprising, after the way you have prospered him. Everything he touches turns to gold. Let something happen to his wealth and see how righteous he'll be."

"All right," the Lord says, "you can do anything you want to him, but you can't touch him personally."

The scene shifts to earth, where Job loses his fortune in a single day. Marauders steal his flocks, and his children are slain; only his dreadful wife remains. But the Scripture says that in all of this Job did not sin or blame God.

Again the scene shifts to heaven and the Lord speaks to Satan, "I think Job did rather well under the circumstances, don't you?"

"I'm not surprised," Satan says. "You drew such a wall around him. Let something touch his own skin and then see how righteous he'll be."

"All right, Satan, you can do anything to Job you want, but you can't take his life."

Back on earth, poor Job breaks out in boils from the top of his head to the bottom of his feet, sitting on an ash heap in total misery, scraping himself with a piece of broken pottery. On top of that, his wife comes along and says, "Why don't you curse God and die?"

Yet Job does not sin with his lips, the Scripture says.

And that's the point we need to see. Job, equated in literature throughout the earth with the troubled human, the man of great suffering and patience, was governed by God. It was He who regulated the severity of Job's troubles. The evil one could go only as far as the Lord permitted, and the temptation failed. Job ultimately was restored to unprecedented prosperity as his trust in God's faithfulness remained steadfast.

We see this in the exodus of the children of Israel from Egypt. God chose to lead them in a very roundabout way right into an apparent trap at the Red Sea when He could have led them another way. He was teaching them dependence upon Him, and it was a severe trial.

Then there was the desperate need for food. What a trial and temptation! But He provided.

There was the need for water. He provided.

One trial, one test after another, all to teach them dependence upon Him.

What does this show us about the Lord's Prayer and our desire to live in the will of God? It convinces me I cannot promise you that when you pray, "Lead us not into temptation" you will never have another temptation. That would be a lie. If the Lord answered the prayer that way, you would stop growing in your faith.

No, by making that petition you are not to expect that in this life you will reach the state where you are no longer tempted. It is not God's will that you should achieve that state of living, for you would lose all sense of your need for Him.

He knows how weak we are and how so often we develop the illusion we are strong. Do you remember how strong you felt right after your conversion or your first awareness of it? You probably experienced that period when things you'd struggled with for years seemed to melt away and you thought, "Wow, I will never be tempted like that again!" Before long, you had a confidence that very subtly became based on yourself and not the Lord. And God had to let you crash, in a sense—to be brought to the place of temptation and trial where you once again perceived your great need for Him.

Remember, though, God does not tempt; He tests. Unfortunately some of the newer translations of Scripture make the Lord's Prayer read, "Do not bring us to the test." If that were answered, we might never fully learn of God's faithfulness.

When we pray, "Lead us not into temptation but deliver us from evil," we are voicing an awareness of our frailty. He does not want us to try to escape the pressures of life, although that is a natural inclination. He wants us to pray that we will be strengthened in our desire not to *fall* to the pressures, for if that is our sincere desire, we will *not* fall. "Lead us not *into* the temptation—into *desiring* it, *succumbing* to it," we might say. The preposition is important. For He will lead us *to* temptation but will not allow us to be tested beyond our ability to withstand. He will deliver us.

> *When* you pass through the waters
>   I will be with you;
> and through the rivers, they shall
>   not overwhelm you;
> *when* you walk through fire you shall
>   not be burned,
> and the flame shall not consume you.
> For I am the Lord your God,
>   the Holy One of Israel, your *Savior*.[14]

Note that it does not say *"if* you pass through the waters" or *"if* you walk through fire," but rather "when." This causes us to see the Lord's meaning in this petition with a paraphrase: "Father, when You lead us *to* temptation and trial, do not let us fall *into* the clutches of it, but take us *through* it. Deliver us from the intentions of Satan."

---

14. Isaiah 43:2-3

AND LEAD US NOT INTO TEMPTATION

* * *

I was taken by a friend on a tour of a test facility of a major airplane manufacturer in Seattle. We arrived at a huge hangar. Inside, along one wall, were rows of rooms containing mysterious computers and machines. From one of the rooms my friend and I looked out into the vast open area of the hangar, and suspended there was a beautiful, futuristic-looking plane, glistening in the reflection of a thousand lights.

My friend, an official of the facility, told me to watch the plane. He pulled a lever and I heard a roar, realizing then that I was looking into a wind tunnel. The roar increased; it was deafening.

"Watch the plane," he said above the roar.

I couldn't believe what I was seeing. The plane's fuselage began to twist and bend as though it were paper, and the wings flapped. He kept pushing the lever. I felt like screaming. *You'll tear it to pieces,* I thought.

Finally, he eased back the lever, and the pressure reduced. The computers were working madly, setting down a record of what had happened.

And what had happened? My friend and his crew had tested that plane by putting it under pressure to reveal any weak spots.

Instantly I had an image of God working with His people. He continually tests us, knowing Himself where the weak spots are but allowing the pressure to build to where we can see them and realize our dependence upon Him to keep us from blowing apart. Only then can we strengthen those weak spots with His help. Like the men with the computers, He knows how far we can go without breaking.

That is what we remember when we pray, "Lead us not into temptation, but deliver us from evil."

* * *

How long does the Lord allow this process to go on?

A story helps to answer. It involves a rock collector. He collected beautiful stones from everywhere, and then he polished them in a machine that made them very beautiful. It was really a rather simple process. The stones were put into the machine together and it went around and around, throwing them together, knocking off the rough edges, so slight as to be almost invisible, until the stones sparkled. They shone because of the constant interaction with the rest of the stones in the machine.

One day a man asked the collector, "How do you know when you've polished a stone long enough?"

The collector smiled, and said quietly, "When I can see my reflection in it."

That's the way it is with God. He lets us be tempted until that area of our lives with which He is concerned has been brought under His control, and He can see the Lord Jesus in it. Then no further testing, no more polishing, is necessary.

⊱ Nine ⊰

For Thine Is the Kingdom and the Power and the Glory, For Ever

THE LORD'S PRAYER is its original form probably ended with "...and deliver us from evil." But during the early Christian era, perhaps within the first two centuries, this sentence was added:

> For Thine is the kingdom, and the power,
> and the glory, for ever.

We have some 6,000 full or partial manuscripts of the New Testament from early times, and in about half of the most ancient ones, this tradition is found in some form. My view is that, if Jesus didn't say it, He very well could have, because it harmonizes perfectly with what we have already examined and brings the prayer full circle. For it begins with worship and praise in the hallowing and exalting of the Lord and concludes by ascribing all sovereignty, all might and all majesty to Him in a triune expression of praise.

Thus the Lord's Prayer—Christ's instructions for our prayers and lives—is a perfectly wrought unity. One might say Jesus described prayer as "petition sandwiched between worship."

*   *   *

Thine is the kingdom. The Scriptures speak hundreds of times of the king and the kingdom, including this powerful illustration from the Psalms:

> *The Lord reigns:* He is robed in majesty;
>   the Lord is robed, He is girded with strength.
> Yea, the world is established; it shall never
>   be moved;
> *Thy throne* is established from of old;
>   Thou art from everlasting.
> The floods have lifted up, O Lord,
>   the floods have lifted up their voice,
>   the floods lift up their roaring.
> Mightier than the thunders of many waters,
>   mightier than the waves of the sea,
>   the Lord on high is mighty!
> Thy decrees are very sure;
>   holiness befits Thy house,
>   O Lord, for evermore.[1]

When we pray, "Thine is the kingdom," we declare, "Lord, You reign; You are sovereign over all the earth."

But do we really *believe* God is absolutely sovereign in all the earth? Do we deep down believe He is in control of the world and all its tiniest details—even when it appears to be falling apart? Do we believe He is, again in the words of J. B. Phillips, "big enough" to handle the job?[2]

The viewpoint of Scripture is that God governs everything; kings rise and fall at His behest, nations are limited in what they can do. There is no suggestion of a dualism

1. Psalm 93
2. *Your God Is Too Small*, by J. B. Phillips

with God and Satan struggling for dominance in a battle whose end is uncertain.

The wonderful, but sadly misunderstood book of the Revelation teaches the proper way to view the world. John, the author, was invited in the Spirit into the throne room of the universe and from that perspective described the world and our lives in numerous visions, often overlapping and not necessarily chronological. Many times in his visions things seem to be in total chaos, so much so that we want to cry out, "God, where are You in all of this?" But John said, in essence, that this was merely the way it looks until we grow accustomed to that perspective.

The point that becomes absolutely clear is that there is no uncertainty about how things will turn out. God is sovereign. He wins. He created a world in which evil was possible, but it exists only with His permission and to accomplish His purpose.

Finally, when we pray, "Thine is the kingdom," we are not simply noting that God is sovereign; we are capitulating to that sovereignty. We are surrendering our own rival kingdoms. We are saying, "Father, I don't want to be the lord of my life; I want You to be my Lord."

*　　*　　*

Thine is the power. Do you really believe all power resides in the hand of God? That is what is proclaimed here.

Do you believe that the power, the influence, the control you have are given to you and don't originate with you?

It is strange that the things in which we usually take pride are the things we have the least power to bring about. People take pride in their beauty, their handsomeness, and yet they did not create those qualities. Some are proud of their wealth and possessions, but the Bible reminds us:

"Beware lest you say in your heart, 'My power and the might of my hand have gotten me this wealth.' You shall remember the Lord your God, for *it is He who gives you power to get wealth...*" [3]

Consider your skills and talents. Scripture says, in the parable of the talents[4] and Moses' experience in the building of the tabernacle,[5] that our abilities are given to us, entrusted to us, to be developed and used for the glory of God.

Consider the fact that you are alive right now. The instinctive reaction is to say your life was your parents' idea. But that's not true. The most they had in mind was a child, a son or a daughter, but they really did not have *you* in mind—that combination of personality and temperament, strength and weakness that makes up you. God gave you life, and He fashioned you, made you a center of consciousness. You had nothing to do with it. You are here, right where you are, by divine appointment. Why weren't you born a thousand years ago or a thousand years hence? Because God chose for you to be here now.

Thine is the power. His is the power to give and to withhold life. That is why life, your life, is of such consequence. No one walking this globe has an unimportant life. Maybe he was an accident, an afterthought, as far as his parents are concerned, but never as far as God is concerned. And that invests every life with a special dignity, which is a message the entire world needs to hear.

When we pray, "Lord, to you is all power," we tie this together with "Thine is the kingdom." That says, "Thine is the power that will bring about the kingdom." If we don't believe that, we shouldn't even bother to pray.

The kingdom is not going to come through our own efforts, nor is the Lord wiping His brow far off in heaven and wondering if we're going to make it. One of the great

3. Deuteronomy 8:17-18
4. Matthew 25:14-30
5. Exodus 35:30-36:1

lessons of the New Testament is that God is able to finish that which He began.[6] We humans can start things and get them rolling, and then they collapse. Not so with God.

Finally, *Thine is the glory*.

Everything is for the glory of the Lord. *We* are for the glory of the Lord. St. Paul wrote:

> ...we who first hoped in Christ have been destined and appointed to live for the praise of His glory.[7]

In this regard, we are like the moon in reference to the sun. This shone through clearly for me one cold, crisp December night when the moon over Darien seemed perfectly full, round and bright. It illuminated the entire landscape. And yet the moon had no light of its own. It was inert, dead. But it marvelously reflected the sun and shed its light abroad.

We humans are made in the same way—to reflect the Lord God, to live our lives in the praise of His glory. If our lives have any glory, it is a reflected glory from the Source of all light and life.

Here is how Jesus described His relationship to the Father:

> "I glorified Thee on earth, having accomplished the work which Thou gavest Me to do..."[8]

How did He glorify God? "By finishing the work You gave Me." What does this say about us? It declares a central fact about the Christian life: there is no way to glorify God other than to do His will. We can't glorify Him on our terms. Jesus did it by accomplishing what He had been given to do. We must do the same.

*   *   *

6. Philippians 1:6
7. Ephesians 1:12
8. John 17:4

At Christmastime we talk and sing of the Son of God who emptied Himself of His glory and came into the world as a servant, born in a stable—where there certainly is very little glory, despite what most Christmas cards show. Stables, especially those in the Middle East, just aren't clean and tidy, shining with light. And that's where Jesus came. His glory was not really manifest, at least not to many. In fact, only once in His natural lifetime did His glory break forth, and even then only a few saw it. That occurred on what we call the Mount of Transfiguration, and St. John, who was there, told of beholding "His glory, glory as of the only Son from the Father."[9] Except for that moment of transfiguration (see Matthew 17:1-8), Jesus was without the glory that had been His.

So, on the night before His crucifixion, He prayed, "Father, glorify Thou Me . . . with the glory which I had with Thee before the world was made."[10] And then He added this:

> ". . . The glory which Thou hast given Me I have given to them . . . (and) Father, I desire that they also, whom Thou hast given Me, may be with Me where I am, to behold My glory which Thou hast given Me in Thy love for Me before the foundation of the world."[11]

He wants His people to behold His glory and, more than that, to share in that glory, that they may live in the unimaginable fullness of light and holiness.

"If you would pray rightly," Jesus said, "then ascribe to your Father all the kingdom, all the power and all the glory, and desire that this would be shown forth in your lives."

---

9. John 1:14
10. John 17:5
11. John 17:22-24

❧ Ten ❧

Amen

WE ARRIVE AT the last word. And whether it was in the original prayer or was added by the early Christians, it has profound significance that Jesus wants us to see.

Amen.

For many, it's the emptiest word of a prayer. They see it as a sort of "Roger, over and out," a polite way of saying, "Okay, Lord, I'm done now; good-by." And that wouldn't be so tragic except for the misunderstanding about prayerful life that it betrays. Why would anyone bother to pray if his relationship to God was one in which he talked to Him for a couple of minutes and then simply walked away from the relationship to get on with other things? But that's what "amen" signifies for so many.

The word itself is Greek—*amen*—And can be translated "verily" or "truly." If you looked at the Greek text of one of the passages where Jesus said, "Verily, verily," it would read, "Amen, amen." The dictionary describes it as a word "used to express solemn ratification or hearty approval." A more precise English equivalent is "let it be so" or "so be it." Thus, when we say or hear a prayer and add the amen, individually or collectively, we are saying, "Yes, this is right; I agree. Let this happen; let this be the case."

You will recall how the Virgin Mary spoke her amen to the angel of the Lord:

"Behold, I am the handmaid of the Lord; let it be to me according to Your word."[1]

I have a banner on a wall at home that makes the point perfectly. It says, "The Christian's response is amen." Our whole life should be a response to God. He initiates.

Remember, Abraham didn't sidle up to God and suggest they get together. The Lord initiated the move to call out a people; Abraham said amen. And the pattern has continued. "You did not choose Me," Jesus said to His disciples, "but I chose you . . ."[2] St. John reminds us, "We love, because He first loved us."[3]

The older I get in my walk with Christ, the more I see that I don't want to change His will. I don't want to persuade Him to my view. I don't want Him to bless the deliberations of my mind and the work of my hands. I want whatever is in the recesses of His heart for my life.

Thus "amen" is my name. I begin each day with words like these: "What do You have in mind this day, Lord? What do You want to bring to me? Let it be to me according to Your word." Following this I can be confident that I will walk through that day in the will of God. As I praise Him, as I seek first His kingdom, as I trust Him for every need, as I receive forgiveness, as I triumph through temptation, He will work out the details of my life according to His purpose. He wants to do it even more than I want Him to.

1. Luke 1:38
2. John 15:16
3. I John 4:19

That approach certainly simplifies one's prayers. I find I do less instructing and more yielding. God is Lord, and I am "amen." For, as St. Paul teaches,[4]

> ... the Son of God, Jesus Christ, whom we preached among you ... was not Yes and No ...

Are you one of those people who can't give a flat answer? I meet them all the time. "Yes," they say, "but on the other hand ..." Or, "Well, yes, I guess so." Jesus wasn't that way, according to Paul. With Him, it was always yes.

> ... For all the promises of God find their Yes in Him. That is why we utter the Amen through Him, to the glory of God.

And that is what we are saying when we simply utter "amen" to the pearls of promise lying just beneath the surface of the Lord's Prayer. Our lives have found their "yes" in Christ. That is the will of God for us.

---

4. II Corinthians 1:19-20

Father,

True prayer, true worship, is not a matter of words only; it arises from the yielding of our lives, the surrendering of our kingdoms to Your conquest of love. For myself, Lord, I ask You to tear down any flag of conquest that I have raised over any area of my life. I yield it in unconditional surrender to You, my Father. I don't want to be the lord or the ruler of my life or the lives of others. I simply want Your kingdom to be established in my life and in my home and in all that concerns me. I want to live fully in Your will, and I so dedicate myself right now. I trust that You will, according to Your word, cause me both to will and to do Your will.

I thank You for the words of my Lord Jesus Christ that reveal this path to the center of Your purpose. I thank You for the Lord's Prayer and for all the Holy Scriptures which so wonderfully set forth Your plan for creation. I thank You for that plan itself.

Amen.

ABOUT THE AUTHORS

EVERETT L. (Terry) FULLAM is pastor of one of the fastest growing congregations in America, St. Paul's Episcopal Church in Darien, Connecticut. He is a dynamic teacher and speaker whose special gift of music has made him popular at conventions and seminars in many denominations and in foreign countries. In addition to his pastoral concerns in Darien, he leads a weekly Monday Bible study in Washington, D.C., that has added to the spiritual life of the nation's capital. Although *Living the Lord's Prayer* is his first book, another book, *Miracle in Darien* tells the fascinating story of a small New England parish transformed into a beacon of spiritual renewal.

BOB SLOSSER is the author of several books, including the best-selling *The Miracle of Jimmy Carter*. A former news editor for *The New York Times*, Slosser serves on the board of the Christian Broadcasting Network and is a member of St. Paul's in Darien.